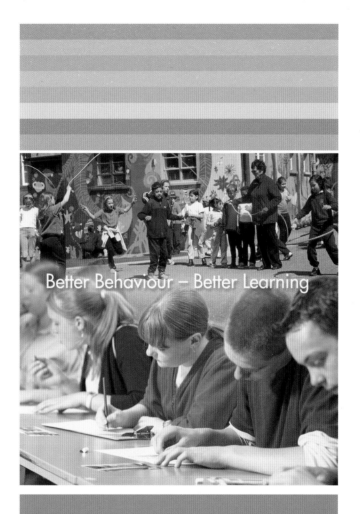

Better Behaviour – Better Learning

Report of the Discipline Task Group

19 June 2001

contents

JACK McCONNELL, MSP

Minister for Education, Europe and External Affairs

and Chair of the Discipline Task Group

Dear Colleagues

I am pleased to be able to introduce the report of the Discipline Task Group that I established in December 2000.

Ensuring good discipline in our schools is a top priority for me – and for Scotland's pupils and their parents/carers. All children and young people should experience education of the highest quality in a secure environment, free from distraction and disturbance

In listening to the views of teachers throughout the national negotiations on teachers' pay and conditions of service, I was struck by the level of concern about pupil indiscipline. This should be a cause for concern for us all. We must now establish a coherent framework for action which supports the work of schools in promoting effective learning and teaching through a positive and purposeful ethos of achievement.

It is very important to support the needs of children and young people who often, for understandable reasons, feel alienated and whose outward behaviour can often disrupt, not only their own education, but that of many other pupils. However, in achieving this goal we must also ensure that the education of the vast majority of our pupils, who are in the main pleasant, hardworking and committed, is of the highest standard.

Balancing these needs is not easy – there are no straightforward solutions. However, there are many encouraging and promising initiatives already underway in individual schools and local authorities across Scotland.

I want to pay tribute to the work and commitment of the Discipline Task Group in producing their report within the deadline I set. I am confident that their findings and recommendations will be of benefit to all those in education who have an interest in working with children and young people. There was extensive consultation with teachers, pupils, parents and a wide range of other professionals and interested parties. I am grateful to all those who helped inform our decision-making and to Neal McGowan, who acted as Secretary of our Group.

There will now be an Action Plan for implementation and I hope to see all schools with refreshed policies in place over the coming year. I want those policies to be supported by parents and pupils, to be backed up by the local authorities and to be enthusiastically implemented by staff in our schools. If we all now work together to achieve change and improvement, we can make a real difference in the months and years ahead.

JACK McCONNELL, MSP

19 June 2001

summary of recommendations

	Scottish Executive	Local Authorities	Schools
1	The Scottish Executive should provide guidance to all schools on the degree of curricular flexibility available within current guidelines to enable them to take account of local circumstances and meet individual pupil needs. (p17)	✓		
2	Local authorities and schools should review existing policies and guidelines relating to learning and teaching, making explicit links with policies for promoting positive discipline. It is recommended that these should be integrated into a single framework of effective inclusive practice. (p19)		✓	✓
3	The additional resources already agreed and planned to support schools and education authorities through the implementation of *A Teaching Profession for the 21st Century*, and for the continuation of the classroom assistants and class size strands of the Excellence Fund should be prioritised to increase staffing (teaching and non-teaching) in order to support social inclusion and the development of positive discipline strategies in all schools. (p19)	✓	✓	✓
4	Schools should agree and share good practice on routine procedures for managing pupils in and around the school and within classrooms. These procedures should be applied consistently by all staff. (p22)			✓
5	The Scottish Executive should endorse the principles of staged intervention. Funding should be made available to enable a number of pilot programmes on staged intervention to be established. The evaluation of such programmes should pay particular attention to the links between indiscipline, classroom management and effective learning and teaching. (p25)	✓	✓	✓
6	Schools should agree and adopt policies for the management of pupil care, welfare and discipline, including the promotion of positive behaviour. Particular attention should be paid to expectations, rules, rewards and sanctions. These policies should be applied consistently. (p28)			✓
7	Local authorities should provide support and advice for all schools in the formulation of policies relating to pupil care, welfare and discipline. School policies and their implementation should be regularly reviewed and endorsed by the local authority and these arrangements should be evaluated by HM Inspectorate of Education through their inspections of education authorities. (p28)		✓	✓
8	A national mechanism for identifying, evaluating and disseminating good practice at education authority and school levels should be established and funded. As part of this mechanism, national research focused on school discipline, behaviour management and school inclusion should be developed. (p28)	✓		
9	In supporting the concept of creating a 'learning community', schools should consult with pupils, teachers and parents/carers in order to agree a dress code for children and young people. Local authorities should support schools in the implementation of their agreed dress codes. (p30)		✓	✓

	Scottish Executive	Local Authorities	Schools
10	In consultation with schools, the Scottish Executive and local authorities should consider how additional and existing funding might be used to provide auxiliary support to assist with the care and welfare of children and young people. Consideration should be given to appropriate training for these staff. (p30)	✓	✓	
11	Local authorities should provide guidance and advice to all staff regarding the levels of intervention they expect from them with respect to their handling of disciplinary matters in classrooms and public areas within the school. (p31)		✓	
12	Schools should develop agreed systems for shared responsibility between staff at all levels for the conduct and behaviour of children and young people in corridors, playgrounds and public areas within the school. (p31)			✓
13	Schools should ensure that there are formal mechanisms in place to allow all pupils to regularly share their views with teachers and other pupils, and to participate in decision-making on matters which affect them directly. These mechanisms should allow for consultation and active participation on a range of issues, including the setting of priorities for the school development plan. (p34)			✓
14	Schools should ensure that opportunities are provided for senior pupils at both primary and secondary levels to take responsibility for 'buddying' and/or mentoring junior pupils. (p34)			✓
15	Schools should review the mechanisms and approaches used to communicate with and involve parents/carers in the general life of the school and with their own child's education in particular. (p36)			✓
16	A national development programme on parenting skills should be developed. (p36)	✓		
17	The Scottish Executive and local authorities should prioritise funding from within the Excellence Fund to provide for a home-school links worker in secondary schools and primary clusters. (p37)	✓	✓	
18	A media campaign focusing on parents'/carers' rights and responsibilities in the school system should be established. This should include an information leaflet for parents/carers highlighting these rights and responsibilities, and advising ways to support their child's education. (p37)	✓		
19	Schools should give consideration to integrating the work of learning support, behaviour support and guidance into a single overall framework of pupil support in order to achieve a more holistic approach to supporting the needs of all children and young people. (p39)			✓
20	There should be a review of the criteria and formula for the allocation of learning support staffing to all schools to allow for appropriate levels of support for children and young people with special educational needs, including those with social, emotional and behavioural difficulties. (p39)	✓	✓	

	Scottish Executive	Local Authorities	Schools
21	There should be a comprehensive review of the nature and purpose of guidance, both at primary and secondary school levels, and of the training of guidance staff. (p40)	✓	✓	
22	Flexible support provision, including in-class support and facilities to educate children and young people outwith the normal classroom environment, should be established in secondary schools and designated primary schools. Best practice in operating such provision should be further researched and disseminated nationally. (p42)	✓	✓	✓
23	In planning for new and refurbished school buildings, local authorities should seek to ensure that suitable and appropriate accommodation is made available for supporting the needs of children and young people who may need to be educated outwith the normal classroom environment. They should also consider how to adapt existing school buildings to allow this to happen. (p43)		✓	
24	The guidance contained within Circular 2/98 *Guidance on Issues Concerning Exclusion from School* should be reviewed in the light of the Standards in Scotland's Schools etc. Act 2000. Local authorities should ensure that all schools are aware of relevant guidance and legislation relating to exclusions from school. As part of their inspections of education authorities, HM Inspectorate of Education should review the procedures used to manage the process of exclusions from school. (p44)	✓	✓	
25	All schools should have a designated member of staff who is responsible for the care, welfare and tracking of progress of looked after children. There is a clear role for this member of staff in supporting colleagues in caring for the interests and welfare of looked after children. (p45)			✓
26	There should be joint multidisciplinary decision-making relating to the care and welfare of children and young people experiencing social, emotional or behavioural difficulties. Clear mechanisms for ensuring effective multidisciplinary working, adapted to meet local needs and circumstances, should be established for all nursery, primary and secondary school clusters to provide holistic and responsive support for children, young people and their families as required. (p48)		✓	✓
27	Schools and local authorities should consider how to further enhance their investment in early intervention strategies aimed at pre-school and primary school children and their families. This should include a specific focus on supporting pupils with social, emotional and behavioural difficulties which encompasses local family support strategies. (p52)		✓	✓
28	Local education authorities and schools should review policies and procedures to ensure all educational transitions, including those between mainstream education and alternative provision, are proactively managed in the best interests of all children, young people and families. (p52)		✓	✓

	Scottish Executive	Local Authorities	Schools
29	The success strategies identified in the New Community Schools pilot should be rolled out to secondary schools and primary schools across Scotland. (p53) ✓		
30	As trusted professionals, all teachers should have access to relevant background information on pupils, including personal and family details, which may affect the learning and teaching process. (p56)		✓
31	The current review of initial teacher education should include the extent to which student teachers are prepared to meet the challenges of supporting social inclusion through effective behaviour management, the promotion of positive discipline and classroom management skills. It should also include the development of opportunities for students following ITE courses to link with professionals in other fields and to develop an awareness of approaches to working with parents and carers. (p57) ✓		
32	In partnership with teacher education institutions and faculties of education, a national continuing professional development programme relating to behaviour management, social inclusion, alternatives to exclusion and effective learning and teaching for probationers, serving teachers and senior managers should be developed. (p58) ✓	✓	
33	The continuing professional development programme should include opportunities for teaching staff to take part in multidisciplinary training with professionals in other fields and to develop an awareness of approaches to working with parents and carers. (p59) ✓	✓	
34	The Scottish Executive should develop a set of policy targets linked to the performance measures within the National Priorities, focused on school ethos and discipline. These should support education authorities and schools in maintaining a greater number of children and young people with social, emotional and behavioural difficulties within mainstream schools without adversely affecting the progress or welfare of other pupils or staff. Schools should receive appropriate funding to achieve such targets. (p61) ✓		
35	The relevant strands of the Excellence Fund should be reviewed and focused on promoting effective learning and teaching, promoting positive discipline and alternatives to exclusion. (p61) ✓		
36	There should be a national strategy developed to manage the implementation of the recommendations offered by the Discipline Task Group. Local authorities and schools should also consider how they can best address the recommendations which apply directly to them. HM Inspectorate of Education should review the progress being made by local authorities and schools in this respect through routine inspections. (p62) ✓	✓	✓

1

introduction

There is a wide range of views about the level of indiscipline in schools, what counts as indiscipline and what should be done about it. These views need to be set within the context of both legislative requirements and professional commitments relating to the education and welfare of children and young people.

Background

1.1 In December 2000 the Minister for Education, Europe and External Affairs, Jack McConnell, announced the establishment of a short-life Discipline Task Group (DTG) in response to concerns expressed over indiscipline in Scottish schools. Membership of the DTG is shown in Appendix 1. Our remit, shown in Appendix 2, was to recommend strategies to the Scottish Executive aimed at securing purposeful and orderly conditions in schools to allow those involved in education to participate positively and appropriately in the processes of learning and teaching.

1.2 The report is based on evidence gathered from a wide range of sources. An extensive programme of consultation was undertaken and the DTG heard evidence from expert witnesses, individuals, groups and numerous professional organisations. In open seminars across Scotland, 600 teachers met directly with members of the DTG to discuss their views and opinions on school discipline and how it might be better managed for the benefit of all members of the school community. Pupils' views were expressed through questionnaires – all 32 local education authorities were invited to involve pupils from primary and secondary schools in participating in open discussions about indiscipline from their perspective, and the outcomes of these were forwarded to the DTG. In addition, a range of opinion was submitted through a dedicated website.

1.3 In gathering evidence for this report we were made aware of a wide range of causes of indiscipline and suggested strategies for improving it. We take the view that if there was a straightforward answer to the problem of indiscipline in schools, someone would have discovered it by this stage. Our work has highlighted the complex nature of indiscipline and has concluded that there is no single overall solution which can solve all problems. Our recommendations focus on:

- the inescapable links between good discipline and effective learning and teaching
- positive participation by all members of the school community in decision-making on all matters which affect them
- multidisciplinary working which can bring a range of skills, expertise, experience and commitment to working with children and young people who have social, emotional or behavioural difficulties.

1.4 We recognise the difficulties and challenges faced by teachers and related professionals in the field of education. We consider that progress is most likely to be made if schools, as learning communities, are supported in establishing local solutions to local circumstances. It is clear that 'solutions' to indiscipline cannot be grafted from elsewhere onto a school's own context and culture. Staff, pupils, parents/carers and others must be involved in key decision-making and have a stake in the processes and procedures adopted. As a result, our recommendations feature key issues and principles which the Scottish Executive, local authorities and schools may wish to consider when developing policy. We hope and believe this provides an effective framework for improvement.

1.5 A shared value base is an important prerequisite in promoting positive behaviour and in reacting to discipline problems when they occur; values underpin practices. For example, a range of studies has revealed the close connection between the beliefs of the senior management team in a school and its exclusion rates. Schools where senior staff had a strong commitment to the social as well as the academic purposes of education tended to have lower exclusion rates.

National priorities

1.6 In forming our key principles, we looked to the Scottish Executive's National Priorities in education, established by the improvement framework within the Standards in Scotland's Schools etc. Act 2000, requiring Scottish Ministers and local authorities to endeavour to secure improvement in the quality of education in Scotland's schools. The National Priorities are defined under the following headings:

- achievement and attainment
- framework for learning
- inclusion and equality
- values and citizenship
- learning for life.

1.7 The current priorities, as laid out in *The Education (National Priorities) (Scotland) Order 2000* are listed in Appendix 3.

Key principles

1.8 Key principles which support the promotion of a positive learning environment were identified by the DTG as being:

The purpose of education

Section 2(1) of the Standards in Scotland's Schools etc. Act 2000 requires that education is to be directed 'to the development of the personality, talents and mental and physical abilities of the child or young person to their fullest potential.' Learning abilities and life skills are both important and complementary, and children and young people should have opportunities to develop different kinds of abilities and experience success within multiple contexts.

The experiences children and young people gain throughout their education must provide them with the life skills required to equip them to participate safely, purposefully and positively in an increasingly complex world. Schools have a key role to play in nurturing young people's core skills to support them through childhood and in later life.

Effective learning and teaching

Effective learning and teaching is much easier to achieve where a positive ethos and good discipline prevail. Discipline policy cannot, and should not, be separated from policy on learning and teaching – the two are inextricably linked. Children and young people are more likely to engage positively with education when careful consideration is given to the factors which affect their learning and teaching.

Entitlement to education

All children and young people are entitled to permanent, full-time education of the highest quality which enables them to develop as individuals and gain skills, knowledge and understanding – however that may be organised. Access to education is a key element in determining life chances. They are also entitled to have the opportunity to gain qualifications – denial of this reinforces disadvantage in our society.

If pupils are educated in a well-ordered and structured environment, these entitlements are enhanced. It is important that these opportunities are not denied to the majority of children and young people as a result of the negative effects of a small minority of troublesome pupils.

Encouraging positive behaviour

Children and young people should learn in an environment which offers well-judged praise and recognition of achievement, and which looks for and focuses on their strengths, takes them seriously and shows a genuine interest in them. Research shows clearly that schools which promote the appreciation and encouragement of the positive contributions of both staff and pupils can be more effective in building motivation, confidence and a sense of responsibility.

Equality and respect

All members of the school community are of equal worth and are entitled to respect. There is no place for discrimination based on race, ethnic origin, religion, gender, sexual orientation, disability, social group or any other grounds. Schools must ensure equality of opportunity and access to education for all children and young people, with particular regard being paid to those learners with disabilities and special needs.

Inclusion

Schools are important public institutions which promote society's values. Children and young people who are part of a educational community and are subject to high expectations of participation, achievement, commitment and personal conduct are more likely to have better long-term opportunities in society as they grow older. They are more likely to continue within the education process, gain purposeful employment and avoid patterns of crime. This is of benefit to them as individuals and to society as a whole.

Participation and citizenship

People are more likely to understand the reasons for policies and procedures, and therefore genuinely subscribe to them, when they have been actively involved in determining them. Participation in decision-making of all staff, children, young people, parents/carers and others is the hallmark of many schools which have been successful in promoting positive discipline.

Partnership working

There is a wide range of factors which affect a person's behaviour, and there is no one way of dealing with the complex problems which can be faced by children, young people and their families. Children's experiences and behaviour in school cannot be disassociated from all other aspects of their lives, including within their families and communities. Accordingly, what happens to children in school is of interest to their parents/carers and involved professionals, and what happens to them in families and communities is of interest to teachers and schools.

In order to develop shared values and understanding of the needs of children and young people, and to maximise the response to those needs, partnership working involving parents/carers, education, social work, health, voluntary agencies and other professions is essential.

2

discipline in schools

The achievements of Scottish education are significant. The majority of young people leave school with qualifications and most are well-rounded individuals. We must ensure that all children experience learning and teaching of the highest quality throughout their time in the education system.

A small number of children and young people have specific behavioural problems which are medical or psychological in origin. However, discipline problems may have their roots in the social and economic challenges faced by families and communities, and sometimes in the way in which the management of learning and teaching is organised. Frequently discipline problems have a variety of causes. Whatever the problems are, they are a barrier to learning and teaching and they must be addressed for the benefit of our young people and society as a whole.

Chapter 2

The context

2.1   In Scotland's schools the majority of children and young people are engaged in quality learning and teaching which is taking place in a positive and purposeful environment. This is essential if they are to attain the highest possible levels of achievement that everyone expects from them. It also helps create an environment in which their values, attitudes and skills can be further developed so that they can face the challenges they meet in a modern society and can embrace the wide range of opportunities open to them after they leave school.

2.2   The achievements of the school system in Scotland in the recent past have been considerable. For instance, in the 1999 examination diet 91 per cent of pupils in S4 gained five or more Standard Grades, and 34 per cent gained five or more Standard Grades at Credit Level. There has been stability in the numbers achieving three or more Highers in S5 – which is the baseline entry qualification for higher education – at 23 per cent of the S4 cohort. Destinations of school leavers now include 32 per cent entering higher education directly, and 19 per cent entering further education. These achievements are testimony to the hard work of pupils and teachers alike.

2.3   However, there are growing concerns regarding the level of indiscipline in our schools. These concerns range from the cumulative effect of low-level indiscipline displayed by routine inappropriate behaviour in classrooms, to the extremely disturbed behaviour exhibited by troubled young people who face major challenges in their lives. There is also concern over the increasing levels of indiscipline and anti-social behaviour witnessed outside the classroom in corridors, playgrounds, dining areas, on school buses and also in areas immediately adjacent to schools.

2.4   No matter what the extent or nature of indiscipline is within any given context or situation, it is a barrier to learning and teaching. Low-level, inappropriate behaviour which typically takes place in classrooms, such as talking out of turn, interrupting others or being inattentive is a nuisance to teachers and pupils alike, and is well recognised as being the most common concern. Evidence suggests that although taken individually most of these misdemeanours are relatively inoffensive, their cumulative effect can damage relationships, prevent appropriate progress in learning and be demoralising for teaching and support staff.

2.5   More challenging behaviour, which can take place both inside and outside the classroom, such as shouting, arguing with teachers, intimidating other pupils or swearing can undermine the ethos and effectiveness of a school. If allowed to persist, it can have long-term damaging effects on pupils' learning, parental confidence in the school, staff morale, and relationships between all three groups. It can also present a barrier to the effective management of the school.

2.6   Seriously disruptive behaviour such as defiance, bullying, aggression and violence can have a seriously detrimental effect on the care and welfare of pupils, teachers and support staff. It is often the case that children and young people exhibiting such seriously disruptive behaviour have deep-seated social and personal problems in other aspects of their lives and are often alienated from school, marginalised and disengaged from the education process.

2.7   Recognition of the continued concern over indiscipline in schools can be illustrated by the number of pupils who continue to be excluded from schools for disciplinary reasons – a number which, in spite of the introduction of the Alternatives to Exclusion grant scheme in 1998, is not reducing. There were 38,769 recorded exclusions from local authority primary, secondary and special schools in Scotland during 1999/2000, a four per cent increase on figures recorded during 1998/99. Eight-five per cent of these exclusions were from secondary schools, 12 per cent from primary schools and three per cent from special schools. (It should be noted that the four per cent increase in exclusions may be in part due to more accurate reporting of exclusions data.)

2.8   It is interesting to note that overall, males accounted for 82 per cent of all exclusions – they accounted for 92 per cent of all primary exclusions and 80 per cent of all secondary exclusions. Gender is clearly an issue in matters relating to school discipline and exclusion. Recent research undertaken by the University of Edinburgh (Tinklin *et al.*, 2001) on behalf of the Scottish Executive has looked closely at gender and pupils performance in Scottish schools. The findings and recommendations from that research should be considered by local authorities and schools in planning learning and teaching.

2.9   The recent report by HM Inspectorate of Education *Alternatives to School Exclusion* (2001) identifies key principles which emerged from the Government's Alternatives to Exclusion grant scheme and offers recommendations which can support schools in becoming more inclusive for all children and young people. The findings contained within that report have helped inform the recommendations made by the Discipline Task Group.

Social factors affecting indiscipline

2.10 We were aware that there are many factors which play a significant part in securing a more inclusive society – factors which may mitigate the best efforts of the various professionals working with children and young people. A background of unemployment, poverty, crime, violence, abuse, alcohol, drugs, mental health and family break up all feature largely in the statistics of young people who experience serious difficulties in school and beyond. Clearly, in facing the challenges of social inclusion, a significant commitment of resources will be required in the area of children's services.

2.11 The views of the DTG concur with the report *Exclusions from Secondary Schools 1995/96* (Ofsted, 1996) that there were a number of factors associated with poor behaviour in school, of which the most significant were that pupils had:

- poor basic skills
- limited aspirations and opportunities
- poor relationships with other pupils, parents/carers or teachers
- pressure from others to behave in a way which may conflict with authority
- parents or carers unable to exercise control
- been exposed to physical or sexual abuse
- been victims of racism.

Social, emotional and behavioural difficulties

2.12 Social, emotional and behavioural difficulties were identified as a source of 'learning difficulties' by the Warnock Report (1978). However, there is no agreement on what counts as a social, emotional or behavioural difficulty – yet such difficulties undoubtedly exist. It is neither possible nor desirable to put labels on children – the problems faced by children experiencing such difficulties will be unique to them. However, pupils experiencing social, emotional and behavioural difficulties undoubtedly take up a great deal of time and energy in schools. They clearly have special educational needs, and as such, should receive support strategies similar to those commonly employed for learning difficulties, including the option of opening a Record of Needs, if necessary.

2.13 Children with behavioural difficulties are often the least liked and least understood of all children with special educational needs. Whether a child 'acts out' (demonstrates bad behaviour openly) or 'acts in' (is withdrawn), they may have barriers to learning which require to be addressed. Children 'acting out' may be aggressive, threatening, disruptive and demanding of attention – they can also prevent other children learning. Children 'acting in' may have emotional difficulties which can result in unresponsive or even self-damaging behaviour. They can appear to be anxious, depressed, withdrawn, passive or unmotivated; and their apparent irrational refusal to respond and cooperate may cause frustration for teachers and other children.

2.14 Children with social, emotional and behavioural difficulties may:

* be unhappy, unwilling and/or unable to work
* receive less praise for their work and have fewer positive child/adult interactions
* have learning difficulties or be under-achieving
* have poor social skills and fewer friends
* have low self-esteem
* be emotionally volatile
* be easily hurt.

School policies

2.15 In listening to the views of teachers, pupils and parents/carers, it seems clear that there are a number of whole-school factors which may work against a positive school ethos and therefore contribute to indiscipline.

2.16 Most schools have developed policies and procedures for managing discipline and many of these policies seem to be working well. However, evidence suggests that some school policies relating to discipline and behaviour management can often be too negative and very bureaucratic – they can create an endless paper chase for staff.

2.17 Good practice in Scottish schools suggests that discipline policies should:

- have a clear set of principles which are developed and agreed by the whole school community
- be concise and avoid unnecessary bureaucracy
- be easily understood by teachers, pupils and parents/carers
- create a sense of ownership for individual teachers and pupils
- focus on positive expectations rather than negative 'rules'
- provide guidelines and support for teachers from the earliest point of concern while retaining flexibility for professional decision-making
- encourage positive parental involvement
- plan for monitoring, evaluation and change
- provide a balance between the needs of the majority and those of the individual child.

2.18 An analysis of these policies suggests that their content includes:

- a statement of ethos and principles
- a description of roles and responsibilities
- a balance between procedures for managing positive rewards and sanctions
- an outline of rules and expectations
- an outline of rewards for achievements
- an outline of sanctions for inappropriate behaviour
- links with and roles of parents/carers
- methods of multidisciplinary working
- procedures for monitoring and evaluation
- clear links to other policies such as

     learning and teaching

     equal opportunities

     learning support

     behaviour support.

Rules, rewards and sanctions

2.19 It makes no sense to devise a universal set of specific rules, rewards and sanctions for all schools. It is quite clear that what is appropriate and works in one setting and context may not necessarily work in another. Like other school policies, discipline systems must evolve and develop over a period of time within a school's own culture and ethos.

2.20 Children and young people generally have no great difficulty with sanctions as long as they are familiar with them, see them to be fairly applied and view them as going hand-in-hand with positive recognition of achievements. It is up to individual schools to decide their rules, rewards and sanctions. However, the DTG has drawn together key principles relating to these which schools should consider when reviewing discipline procedures.

2.21 Rules and expectations should:

- be clear and easy to understand
- be positive in nature and provide opportunities for reward
- reflect the desired ethos and culture of the school
- be fair and acceptable to teachers, pupils and parents/carers
- be comprehensive
- be achievable
- be developed in consultation with pupils, staff and parents/carers.

2.22 Rewards should:

- approve of, recognise and reinforce good behaviour and genuine achievement
- reflect and contribute to the ethos of the school
- reward and motivate children and young people
- encourage children and young people to take responsibility for their own behaviour and achievements
- provide opportunities for parental involvement.

2.23 Sanctions should:

- be immediate and provide the school with opportunities to make appropriate responses to inappropriate low-level behaviour
- include a known range of procedures which come into play when children or young people contravene school expectations
- be fair, appropriate and in proportion to the cause of the sanction
- be applied consistently but take into account individual circumstances
- avoid the humiliation of pupils.

3
promoting better discipline

Some challenges are more difficult to overcome than others. There are steps which schools can take to promote better discipline and therefore improve the conditions for effective learning and teaching to take place. Some schools appear to be making more progress than others in achieving this.

Some measures which can be taken are strategic and can be accomplished reasonably quickly. Others depend very much on the ethos and culture of the school as a learning community. A positive ethos needs to be nurtured and developed over time to bring lasting benefits. The sensitive introduction of praise and reward systems as part of a strategy to develop a positive ethos can bring rapid improvements.

Curriculum and structural issues

3.1   When young people see a purpose to schooling there is less likelihood of them feeling dissatisfied with their education. For many disaffected young people, there may be barriers to learning which can include an inappropriate curriculum, learning difficulties, inappropriate teaching styles and social, emotional and behavioural problems. Consideration should be given to the relevance of the curriculum in meeting the needs of all children and young people and to teaching approaches which facilitate learning for all.

3.2   Scottish education has traditionally been credited with having a system which, in the main, produces young people who are well-educated as a result of having followed a broad and balanced curriculum based on the comprehensive principle. It is essential that all children and young people experience an education system which can develop and strengthen their talents and intelligences over a broad range of areas.

3.3   The following examples illustrate how schools are promoting inclusion through more appropriate curriculum management:

- ensuring breadth and balance across the curriculum through the Core Skills developed as part of the new National Qualifications

- creating greater flexibility of subject choice in S3/S4 for pupils through justified deviations from the modal curriculum structure

- reducing the number of subjects/topics studied in both primary and secondary schools for a small number of children and young people who may have difficulty in coping with a full curriculum

- the use of new National Qualification Units and/or Courses in S3 and S4, particularly at Access 3 and Intermediate 1 in preference to full Standard Grade courses

- the use of alternative curricular experiences for some pupils, for example life skills courses and vocational opportunities linked to further education

- ensuring quality learning and teaching opportunities in personal and social education, education for citizenship, education for work, and out-of-school learning experiences – both in primary and secondary schools

- for some pupils in S4, high-quality work experience and college placements are used in preparation for future training and employment.

3.4   These approaches to curricular flexibility not only support some of the specific needs of pupils with social, emotional and behavioural difficulties, but also a much broader range of pupils who experience boredom and lack of inspiration in school. In order to support schools in taking these creative and flexible steps, consideration should be given to reviewing the mechanisms for measuring attainment in schools. Schools should not see themselves as being disadvantaged in comparison with other schools as a result of catering for a broad range of pupil needs.

recommendation

1.   The Scottish Executive should provide guidance to all schools on the degree of curricular flexibility available within current guidelines to enable them to take account of local circumstances and meet individual pupil needs.

Effective learning and teaching

3.5   It seems clear that where appropriate consideration is given to learning and teaching approaches and where the quality of learning and teaching is consistently high, with the appropriate balance of challenge and support enshrined within an atmosphere of high expectation, discipline problems can be reduced significantly.

3.6   The management of learning and teaching in schools can either assist pupils in managing their behaviour or compound their difficulties. Many schools manage their pupils' behaviour successfully, despite the social and personal difficulties faced by some children and young people. Strategies designed to improve behaviour are most effective when they are linked to effective learning and teaching. Evidence submitted to the DTG focused on a number of key issues which related directly to this.

3.7   Some pupils suggested that they were:

- often bored with the tasks they were assigned
- of the view that some teachers' expectations may not always be high enough
- uninspired by some aspects of the S1/S2 curriculum.

3.8   Teachers suggested that some problems with learning and teaching could be avoided by:

- harnessing the potential of ICT in supporting learning and teaching
- differentiating the curriculum appropriately, particularly for pupils with special educational needs in mainstream classes
- taking account of new knowledge about learning and teaching, including the importance of catering for different learning styles.

3.9   The potential of ICT in reducing barriers to learning has much to offer schools and individual pupils. While ICT appears to feature strongly in the work of all schools, evidence submitted concurs with research showing that it is not always being used to enhance learning. Consideration should be given as to how ICT can support pupils' learning, both generally (eg. in the development of core skills through the use of integrated learning systems) and within subject disciplines.

3.10 To keep children and young people engaged with learning there must be effective differentiation to take account of their individual learning needs. Lessons should be organised to ensure that all pupils receive an appropriate balance of challenge and support. Discipline problems can arise when pupils feel insufficiently challenged and also when they feel insufficiently supported. While it is recognised that effective differentiation is not an easy task, evidence suggests that where account is taken of the learning needs of individual pupils, discipline problems can be reduced. Those who show a high level of ability in a particular area need to be challenged appropriately. Likewise, pupils with learning difficulties should be supported to learn using appropriate materials, tasks and strategies.

3.11 Schools which have incorporated the management of classroom discipline within the policy of learning and teaching under a single framework seem more able to prevent much inappropriate behaviour rather than merely react to it. An effective learning and teaching policy acknowledges that pupils learn in different ways — auditory and visual learning styles being two common examples. Auditory learners learn best by listening and talking — they remember verbal instructions without having to write them down. Visual learners prefer to remember by using their eyes — they appreciate it when teachers use diagrams, pictures and visual presentations to supplement oral discussion. By taking account of different learning styles, teachers can make their teaching more accessible and motivating for pupils.

3.12 To assist schools in doing this, there must be adequate support from the local authority. Like schools, it is important for authorities to develop and agree key principles related to core policies and to share these with schools. Where schools have a sense of ownership in developing these key principles, there is a greater likelihood that they will develop school-based policies linked to them.

r e c o m m e n d a t i o n

2.   Local authorities and schools should review existing policies and guidelines relating to learning and teaching, making explicit links with policies for promoting positive discipline. It is recommended that these should be integrated into a single framework of effective inclusive practice.

3.13 An example of how one authority has approached the task of supporting schools in linking learning and teaching with promoting positive behaviour is Perth and Kinross Council. The case study on page 20 illustrates the approach taken.

Class size

3.14 A repeated concern made to the DTG from teachers, pupils and parents/carers alike was the issue of large class sizes. This is not a straightforward issue to address – there are differing views on what constitutes a class which is 'too large'. For example, if groups are set by attainment, what may be considered reasonable and appropriate for one group of pupils may be wholly inappropriate for another.

3.15 It is also the case that schools may not always consider additional teaching staff to be the appropriate solution to supporting groups of learners. Some schools have developed creative solutions which involve increasing the adult/pupil ratio – but not always with teachers. Well-trained classroom assistants can provide in-class support for all learners and schools can often make a broader impact on learning and pupil welfare by targeting resources in this way.

3.16 We take the view that if staffing resources can be directed at the most challenging situations in all schools, this will have a major impact on learning, teaching and discipline. However, the planning of any additional staffing resources must be long-term to allow schools to be managed effectively. Significant attention given to addressing the current shortage of teachers in some subjects and geographical areas as well as appropriate training and salary structures for classroom assistants.

r e c o m m e n d a t i o n

3.   The additional resources already agreed and planned to support schools and education authorities through the implementation of *A Teaching Profession for the 21st Century*, and for the continuation of the classroom assistants and class size strands of the Excellence Fund should be prioritised to increase staffing (teaching and non-teaching) in order to support social inclusion and the development of positive discipline strategies in all schools.

Case Study

Inclusion through Policy in Perth and Kinross Council

The development of a number of linked, authority-wide policies have helped promote an inclusive model of education and child care provision.

Making a Positive Difference was published in 1999 and reflects the nature of the Council's commitment to developing inclusive practice as the main alternative to excluding young people from school. It identifies key principles and pathways to promoting positive behaviour in our schools. It is widely accepted that schools play a significant part in influencing the behaviour and attainment of pupils, irrespective of the size of school, catchment area or family background. Pupils respond well when they feel secure in a context where they have a sense of being valued and where they have opportunities to succeed. That is not to say that factors outwith school do not influence pupil behaviour, but rather that the school is a major influence and therefore should develop strategies which promote the active participation and commitment of children and young people.

Published in June 2000, *Promoting Positive Learning* draws both on good theory and best practice. It reflects the importance of pedagogy, modern research and development, such as the work of Gardner and Goleman – and is predicted on the principle that confidence and self-esteem are essential ingredients for effective learning and teaching with respect to both young people and teachers.

The guide distills current research and defines key principles for promoting effective learning in our schools. It then discusses the implications of these principles with regard to the learner, the teacher and school management, whilst highlighting pathways from theory into practice in terms of audit and planning for improvement.

Like *Making a Positive Difference*, the guide *Promoting Positive Learning* has been issued to all primary and secondary classroom teachers and support staff across the authority and has been the focus for development within schools, supported by in-service development through the staff development programme.

Promoting and Supporting Inclusive Practice develops the approach to self-evaluation set in out in *How Good is our School?* and in the Quality Management in Education Framework published by the Scottish Executive. This publication is designed to enable all aspects of the integrated services to take forward inclusive approaches to assessing, planning, delivering and reviewing services to young people and their families.

The guide provides a framework which identifies key principles and strategies and draws directly on the Council's commitment to the development of an inclusive model of education and childcare provision. It moves the whole service beyond integration and towards truly inclusive approaches and will be launched formally in August 2001.

Information about these guides is available from
Bryan Paterson, Educational Development Officer,
Education & Children's Services,
Perth and Kinross Council,
Pullar House, 35 Kinnoull Street, Perth, PH1 5GD.

Routine classroom management

3.17 Information from teachers and pupils, both in written evidence and during visits to schools, suggests that where there is consistency and agreement over routine classroom management procedures, children and young people are more likely to understand what is expected of them and follow instructions first time. Some schools have taken the time to review and agree these basic procedures.

3.18 For example, the ways in which pupils are received into the classroom can promote positive behaviour throughout the lesson. In secondary schools, where teachers are present to welcome the class in a calm, orderly fashion and settle them to work quickly, there seems to be an improvement in classroom behaviour. It is important to prevent potentially disruptive and troublesome pupils from congregating in the margins of the room. By preventing this, the teacher is seen to have a high profile and be in control. In primary schools, teachers collecting and accompanying their classes from the playground can have the same effect.

3.19 There is also evidence to suggest that skilled management of the starting of lessons can promote good discipline. For example, leaving the checking of the register and other routine procedures until the class are well on task, rather than delaying the start of the lesson with matters like these, can help promote more focused learning. Similarly, the manner in which latecomers are dealt with can sharpen the start of a lesson. Asking for explanations quietly on a one-to-one basis later in the lesson can be more effective than through a potentially disruptive public challenge at the start.

3.20 It is also clear that pupils respond more appropriately to the tasks set for them when they know what the lesson will contain and what the teacher hopes to achieve. Teachers who share the outline and objectives of the lesson with pupils at the start suggest that this can help foster better concentration and attention.

3.21 Other examples of agreed procedures include whether or not pupils are expected to line up for classes, whether outdoor clothing can be worn in class, etc. These matters are for individual schools to decide. However, it is clearly the case that if there can be consistency across the school on such routine matters there is less likelihood of teachers facing open challenges from pupils over simple requests and instructions.

recommendation

4. Schools should agree and share good practice on routine procedures for managing pupils in and around the school and within classrooms. These procedures should be applied consistently by all staff.

Tackling possible causes of classroom indiscipline

3.22 In listening to the views of teachers, it seems that the 'referral out' style of discipline policy, where the pupil is sent out of the classroom to another teacher, can have inherent weaknesses for long-term improvement in pupils' behaviour. Classroom teachers must be empowered to manage learning and teaching in their own contexts. Children and young people need to see that classroom teachers have authority and responsibility for what happens in their own teaching environments.

3.23 Effective discipline systems are based on supporting classroom teachers in managing pupils' behaviour at classroom level for as long as possible. A system which enables the teacher to retain responsibility and ownership for pupils' behaviour and conduct before referring the situation to other staff has a number of clear advantages:

- the pupils see and identify the teacher as having a locus of control and authority over the situation (this tends to disappear almost as soon as the child is referred elsewhere and so presents even greater problems upon the child's return to the class)

- there is an expectation from pupils that the classroom teacher can resolve difficulties quickly and effectively

- senior staff can support the classroom teacher in an advisory, consultative capacity rather than in a reactive capacity – thus the teacher remains empowered

- it promotes inclusion at classroom level

- it increases the significance to the pupil of finally being referred to the senior staff if and when this eventually happens

- it can reduce hostility amongst pupils

- it reduces time lost to learning and teaching.

3.24 This is not to suggest that teachers are abandoned to look after themselves – quite the opposite. Schools which are making progress in managing behaviour have found ways to support teachers in their natural teaching environments. This support can take the form of:

- advising and assisting with classroom management skills

- providing in-class assistance – sometimes targeting specific pupils or groups

- increasing classroom auxiliary assistance

- assisting with reintegration strategies after pupil absences or exclusions.

3.25 Whatever form the support takes, it seems clear that to empower classroom teachers, they must be seen throughout as the lead person.

Staged intervention

3.26 A discipline policy alone will not provide a school with all the answers to behavioural problems. The inter-relationship of that policy to other policies, particularly those on equality of opportunity, special educational needs and anti-bullying, and more importantly the relationship between policy, practice, organisation and ethos are more likely to produce a climate in which the needs of all can be met.

3.27 Staged intervention provides a structure to support teachers in dealing with behaviour problems. It complements but does not replace the school's discipline system.

3.28 Rather than referring all problems out of the class, a school operating a staged intervention policy analyses approaches to learning, teaching and classroom management to help identify what may be causing some of the problems, and agreeing a plan to tackle them. As the name suggests, interventions are planned in stages in order to establish what is the most appropriate strategy for dealing with the difficulties encountered at any given time.

3.29 The principles of staged intervention include objective and 'can do' approaches, especially in the early response/preventative levels within stage 1. There is an agreement that a problem exists – but no suggestion as to where its root causes lie. For simplicity, staged intervention provides a process covering the full range of behaviours which cause concern – from the child who 'acts out' to the child who is withdrawn. Above all, it offers real *support* rather than blame. Schools operating this system usually have a 'behaviour coordinator' who has responsibility for advising teachers and senior management about approaches to behaviour management at individual class and whole-school levels.

3.30 Staged intervention can be simplified and summarised as follows:

Stage	Action
Stage 1	If a teacher has a concern about a pupil, or a group of pupils, a number of steps can be taken to address this within the class setting. For example, after self-evaluation, some changes might be made to class routines such as the lesson openings, seating arrangements, approaches to question and answer sessions, etc. The class teacher will choose to seek support in analysing and planning the situation with an in-school behaviour coordinator. The planned intervention(s) are tried and evaluated over a number of weeks.
Stage 2	If, after implementing the behaviour environment plan (the planned intervention which focuses on the physical environment of the classroom) over an agreed period of time, the teacher and behaviour coordinator are of the view that the problem may stem from a specific pupil, the focus of the stage two intervention is on that particular pupil. This may involve specific support or interventions planned in conjunction with a learning support or guidance teacher. As the focus is now on the pupil rather than the overall environment, parents/carers may be involved at this stage. The individual plans in stage two may run in conjunction with the planned interventions in stage one.
Stage 3	At this stage, it may be that intensive support is needed for a specific pupil and several agencies may be involved in a more formal way. It may be that an individual educational programme will be drawn up. A small number of children and young people have needs which are very complex and they will require significant professional support throughout their school life. A Record of Needs may be opened for the pupil.

3.31 Staging interventions offers an opportunity for multidisciplinary services to contribute at an early level (stage 1) before situations become critical. The structure of staged intervention forms a common approach to problems and a basis of understanding between the education authority and schools over issues surrounding special educational needs and exclusion.

3.32 A planned model of staged intervention is being developed by East Ayrshire Council. The case study overleaf outlines its principles and how it works.

5.   The Scottish Executive should endorse the principles of staged intervention. Funding should be made available to enable a number of pilot programmes on staged intervention to be established. The evaluation of such programmes should pay particular attention to the links between indiscipline, classroom management and effective learning and teaching.

Helping with audit and planning

3.33 One of the key strands of staged intervention, both at the early levels of classroom audit and planning and also within planned interventions at stages 2 and 3, is the consideration of strategies and approaches which individual teachers and schools may wish to review and implement in an attempt to support learning and teaching. The well-established system of audit in Scottish schools is based on the model adopted in *How Good is Our School?*, which asks the three basic questions: 'How are we doing?'; 'How do we know?'; and 'What are we going to do now?'

3.34 In deciding what to do next, it is essential to know what is working well elsewhere – the sharing of good practice is key to helping schools in reviewing and adapting their policies. One element of this will be through the use of the forthcoming CD-ROM *Dealing with Disruption*, which is due to be launched and supplied to all schools in Scotland in the autumn term of 2001. This brings together a collection of policy, practice and research and provides a set of video, audio and text resources to help teachers consider typical situations where the potential for disruptive behaviour exists and offers advice and support for dealing with it. The project is funded by the Scottish Executive and has been carried out by the Faculty of Education at the University of Edinburgh, with consultancy from the University of Cambridge. There is an obvious role for this interactive resource for both classroom teachers and staff responsible for the coordination of behaviour support in all schools.

Consistency of policy implementation

3.35 Many of the children and young people who responded to the DTG thought lack of consistency from teachers in discipline management was a major contributory factor in encouraging inappropriate behaviour, allowing some pupils to exploit situations and disrupt the experience of others. Some pupils felt that inconsistency brought about a sense of injustice and unfairness. The majority of children and young people indicated that they had no difficulties with the rules and expectations set out in school – their concerns related more to how these procedures were implemented. Staff and pupils both stressed that the key characteristic of effective school discipline was the consistency with which staff, having agreed a policy, apply it over a period of time. A number of staff claimed that their own success was a result of consistency of implementation, combined with a continual review of school policy and practice.

Case Study

Framework for Intervention in East Ayrshire

What is Framework for Intervention (FFI)?

Framework for Intervention is a strategic system which schools can use to help teachers manage low-level classroom disruption which interferes with effective learning and teaching. Originally developed in Birmingham, the model has been adapted to the Scottish context and is being piloted in two secondary schools and five primary schools in East Ayrshire during session 2001/02.

How does FFI work?

The school nominates a member of the teaching staff (at any level) who is trained over a five-day period and becomes the behaviour coordinator (BCo) in that school. The BCo's role is not to sort out all the behaviour difficulties which teachers experience, but rather to support them through the FFI system to develop their own solutions to the problems they are facing in their own classrooms. It gives the individual teacher ownership of the solutions and facilitates learning and teaching within the class. It also has the advantage of being non-prescriptive, yet wholly developmental for the teacher involved. A fundamental principle of FFI is that it is based on an opt-in model, where the relationship between the teacher and the BCo is completely confidential and supportive. It makes no assumptions as to what constitutes a problem for any teacher – if they see a problem, however apparently trivial, then it is a problem. Although FFI is a three-stage strategy, the main focus is always on Stage 1, which seeks to change and manage the learning and teaching environment without any focus on individual children or their problems. Information from the Birmingham project suggests that 80 per cent of referrals are concluded without progressing beyond Stage 1.

Why use FFI?

FFI has all the attributes of a model that is owned and operated by teachers, not imposed from above by management, psychologists or other professionals. Evaluation studies show that it is teachers themselves who highly value FFI and see it as an approach which helps them become better managers of their classroom and hence better teachers. Where it becomes integrated into the ethos and the systems of the school, FFI becomes a fundamental way of working which is wholly consistent with the self-evaluation approaches embedded within *How Good is Our School?*.

Will FFI be effective in our schools?

East Ayrshire as an authority is so encouraged with what FFI appears to offer teachers that they are confident that the principles and practices will transfer effectively into their schools. In order to consider this, there will be a carefully planned evaluation study of the pilot project being carried out by the research psychologists who work with the authority.

How can I find out more about the East Ayrshire project?

Please contact
Tom Williams, Principal Psychologist,
East Ayrshire Council,
Council Headquarters,
London Road, Kilmarnock, KA3 7BU.

3.36 Consistent discipline tends to be found in schools where there is effective leadership, clear planning, supportive behaviour management systems applied across the school, and good use made of evidence from self-evaluation and monitoring. Clear expectations and routines, based on policies and procedures which are agreed, monitored and kept under review are key to improving behaviour.

r e c o m m e n d a t i o n

6. Schools should agree and adopt policies for the management of pupil care, welfare and discipline, including the promotion of positive behaviour. Particular attention should be paid to expectations, rules, rewards and sanctions. These policies should be applied consistently.

r e c o m m e n d a t i o n

7. Local authorities should provide support and advice for all schools in the formulation of policies relating to pupil care, welfare and discipline. School policies and their implementation should be regularly reviewed and endorsed by the local authority and these arrangements should be evaluated by HM Inspectorate of Education through their inspections of education authorities.

3.37 The DTG saw a wealth of high-quality policy and practice in place at classroom, school and authority levels. Some of these initiatives are known and shared; others have an insufficient profile. All schools would benefit from having access to examples of initiatives which are taking place in similar contexts to their own.

r e c o m m e n d a t i o n

8. A national mechanism for identifying, evaluating and disseminating good practice at education authority and school levels should be established and funded. As part of this mechanism, national research focused on school discipline, behaviour management and school inclusion should be developed.

The importance of school ethos

3.38 Evidence from many studies, including case studies from the Scottish Schools Ethos Network, suggests that schools can and do make a difference to the lives of children and young people. Research shows that it is not always schools serving problematic or deprived areas which suffer from the highest levels of indiscipline. It has been demonstrated that a positive, inclusive ethos in which all children and young people are respected and valued is a key characteristic in promoting positive behaviour and reducing exclusions.

3.39 Schools which have been successful in promoting a positive ethos of achievement have focused on the creation and maintenance of good relationships – amongst staff (teaching and non-teaching), pupils and parents/carers. Policies which promote and encourage positive behaviour and participation lie at the heart of building good relationships – both in school and at home.

3.40 Schools which have made progress in developing a positive ethos suggest that pupils take pride in their achievements and recognise the importance of high standards in their work and behaviour. Through a sustained commitment to improving ethos, many schools report having made progress in breaking down the 'it's not cool to be good at school' syndrome, particularly with secondary age males.

3.41 However, it is clear that an ethos of achievement does not come about by chance, nor is it easy to establish in the first place. The role of the head teacher, the senior management team and all staff in promoting a collective atmosphere of care and respect within the formal and informal life of the school community is essential. In order to create this atmosphere, there must be a sense of collective responsibility amongst the staff and a belief that schools can and do make a difference.

School dress code

3.42 A common feature of schools with a positive ethos of achievement is that they have high expectations of their pupils in terms of their behaviour, commitment, participation, academic progress and completion of homework. In many schools with a high ethos of achievement, there has also been a sustained effort to either maintain or introduce a dress code to the school. The benefits of a dress code can be summarised as follows:

- differences between pupils are reduced, which in turn reduces some of the causes of isolation and bullying
- the self-esteem of particular groups of pupils can be improved
- security (particularly in large schools) can be improved – it is easy to spot who does and who does not belong to the school community
- pupils can feel a stronger sense of belonging and commitment to the school
- it can improve the image of the school in the local community
- it can create a sense of purpose within the school environment.

3.43 The DTG take the view that the benefits outlined here, coupled with the experience of schools and authorities which have pursued this, lead us to believe that there is merit in schools giving serious consideration to the continuation or formation of a dress code policy. It is also our view that the nature of the school dress code is for the school community to decide.

3.44 However, while many schools have reported the benefit of promoting a dress code, many have had great difficulty in sustaining its long-term implementation. This requires the continued high-profile emphasis from the school community of the importance of adhering to the agreed dress code policy, which pupils should have had a hand in forming. Schools should agree the dress code with parents/carers, and there should be an expectation both from the school and the education authority, that where there is an agreed dress code, pupils and their parents/carers will support it.

recommendation

9.   In supporting the concept of creating a 'learning community', schools should consult with pupils, teachers and parents/carers in order to agree a dress code for children and young people. Local authorities should support schools in the implementation of their agreed dress codes.

Behaviour outside the classroom

3.45 It was clear from the evidence submitted to the DTG that some of the major concerns over indiscipline were related to situations which take place outside the classroom. Corridor and playground indiscipline, conduct in public areas and on school buses were common examples of the concerns expressed by most respondents. Poor attendance was included in schools' definitions of disruptive behaviour. Absenteeism ranges from skipping individual classes through to prolonged periods of unexplained absence.

3.46 Effective leadership from the head teacher and senior management team is essential in maintaining a positive ethos in and around the school. This includes sharing expectations regularly with staff, pupils and parents/carers. It is also important for senior staff to maintain a friendly high-profile presence throughout the school, particularly during intervals and lunch breaks and at period changeovers in secondary schools, supporting teaching and auxiliary staff in their management of pupil movement and conduct during these times.

3.47 The lack of supervision during lesson changeovers, intervals and lunch breaks can create difficulties for schools. It is often the case that habits and patterns of behaviour developed by pupils outside in public areas can spill into classrooms later.

recommendation

10. In consultation with schools, the Scottish Executive and local authorities should consider how additional and existing funding might be used to provide auxiliary support to assist with the care and welfare of children and young people. Consideration should be given to appropriate training for these staff.

3.48 For a number of reasons, including personal safety and fear of litigation, some classroom teachers may lack confidence in tackling disciplinary matters in public parts of the school. While this is understandable, it is our view that where staff are confident in taking proactive, collective responsibility for children in all parts of the school, there is a greater chance of creating a positive and safer environment for everyone. With the assistance of legal advice, all local authorities should provide schools with guidelines on what they expect from staff in respect of disciplinary interventions in classrooms and public areas. With the knowledge that there is support at school and authority level, staff should be encouraged to maintain a high presence and profile with children and young people in and around the school. There should be a shared responsibility for the care and welfare of all pupils – who should see all teachers as having authority outside their own teaching areas. It is clearly the case that these interventions are most successful when carried out in a positive, encouraging and friendly manner.

recommendation

11. Local authorities should provide guidance and advice to all staff regarding the levels of intervention they expect from them with respect to their handling of disciplinary matters in classrooms and public areas within the school.

recommendation

12. Schools should develop agreed systems for shared responsibility between staff at all levels for the conduct and behaviour of children and young people in corridors, playgrounds and public areas within the school.

4

involving pupils and parents/carers

If people are to engage with improvement strategies, they must feel a sense of ownership as a result of having had a hand in forming them. Many schools, supported by their local authorities, are experimenting with ways of genuinely involving young people and their parents/carers in decision-making about aspects of school life.

This means heightening awareness about rights as well as making a genuine commitment to responsibilities.

Participation of children and young people in decision-making

4.1   The DTG recognises the importance of the involvement and participation of children and young people in all aspects of the decisions which affect their lives and their role as active citizens in our society. This is particularly important where children and young people may be excluded or discriminated against. This is set in the context of the Standards in Scotland's Schools etc. Act 2000, the United Nations Convention on the Rights of the Child – to which the UK Government is a signatory, and the Children (Scotland) Act 1995, where the welfare of the child is paramount.

4.2   Successful schools seek to secure young people's rights to a quality and relevant education by promoting effective approaches to their participation within their school and community, and by embedding citizenship in the learning environment and curriculum. When young people enjoy a positive and meaningful experience in a school which meets their individual needs, treats them with respect and involves them in decision-making, challenging behaviour can be significantly reduced.

4.3   Effective participation by children and young people requires them to have a clear understanding of their rights and responsibilities. Schools play the key role in ensuring that their pupils are provided with the necessary information and guidance to do this.

4.4   There is now a greater emphasis on active citizenship and the empowerment of young people in schools, and this takes many forms. A popular mechanism for ensuring this is through pupil councils, many of which have devolved budgets, where children and young people are elected to represent their peers and contribute to class and whole-school decision-making. A common example of pupil participation in decision-making relates to the promotion of positive behaviour, where children and young people are fully involved in drawing up expectations, rules, rewards and sanctions. Evidence submitted to the DTG suggests that when pupils are involved in this process, they not only feel a greater sense of ownership and commitment to the rules and sanctions, but they also experience school as a place which is fair and treats them with respect and justice. In some of the schools visited it was children and young people who were responsible for managing and coordinating the organisation and allocation of the positive rewards as part of the positive behaviour policy.

4.5   Other examples of active participation include the designing and selection of school dress code, responsibility for fund raising and charity events, and coordinating the invitation of guest speakers and visitors to the school. Section 6 of the Standards in Scotland's Schools etc. Act 2000 requires schools to consult with pupils in attendance at the school over the priorities and content of the school development plan. Schools which view themselves as learning communities, committed to listening to the views of pupils through the creation of a positive ethos, rather than being top-down institutions of discipline and social control appear to achieve more success in establishing positive pupil participation and behaviour.

4.6   The philosophy behind Circle Time or Quality Circles, increasingly being used at all levels, reflects mutual respect and a capacity for children to be given opportunities to talk, share concerns and participate in decision-making. The exchange of views and ideas can cover a range of different topics, including learning and teaching, personal/social relationships and bullying. Circle Time can support the personal and social development of children and young people and it can be an opportunity for them to be heard by other children and adults in a secure and supportive atmosphere.

recommendation

13. Schools should ensure that there are formal mechanisms in place to allow all pupils to regularly share their views with teachers and other pupils, and to participate in decision-making on matters which affect them directly. These mechanisms should allow for consultation and active participation on a range of issues, including the setting of priorities for the school development plan.

4.7   Many teachers and pupils made reference to the success being experienced through the introduction of 'buddy' and mentor schemes, where older pupils support younger children in a range of different issues, including bullying, homework, forming friendships and coping with transitions. These schemes can offer a listening ear and non-threatening support for all children and young people and provide them with a sense of security. There is clear evidence that the young people who take on the role of 'buddy' or mentor also develop skills, experience and confidence which can benefit them and the school.

recommendation

14. Schools should ensure that opportunities are provided for senior pupils at both primary and secondary levels to take responsibility for 'buddying' and/or mentoring junior pupils.

Parental/carer involvement

4.8 Parental/carer involvement in their child's education is critical for encouraging both learning and personal and social development. The DTG was impressed by the strategies schools used to encourage parents/carers to become active participants in school life. We fully recognise that engaging with the most alienated of parents/carers is a challenging task. There are a number of strategies being used by schools to develop more positive relationships with parents/carers. The following list illustrates some practical examples:

- encouraging parent helpers to take part in school outings and other activities
- providing facilities such as a common room as a meeting place for parents/carers
- providing learning opportunities of various kinds for parents/carers and other adults (eg. in the use of ICT)
- regular communication – good news about pupils' achievements, newsletters, etc.
- more flexible parents' consultation events where there is privacy, and where young people attended as a matter of course (eg. some secondary schools have moved to six 'vertical' parents' events per year rather than single 'horizontal' events, thus providing the opportunity for more regular and flexible contact with parents/carers)
- encouraging involvement in parents' organisations
- drop-in clinics operated by senior staff and guidance staff on a regular basis
- involving them in the formulation of the school development plan
- involvement of parent/carer members in school working groups and committees
- linking target-setting initiatives in areas such as attendance, behaviour, punctuality and academic progress to parental commitment events, including the use of high profile commercial/industrial links
- providing employment opportunities in the school, for example as classroom assistants, playground helpers, clerical staff and manual staff.

4.9 Although a requirement for all schools, some are more successful than others in communicating effectively with parents/carers. Schools should inform and seek the support of parents/carers regarding their expectations and policies relating to:

- learning and teaching
- discipline
- care and welfare
- complaints and appeals procedures.

4.10 The DTG believes that when parents/carers are provided with regular, up-to-date and user-friendly information, they are more likely to support the work of the school. Schools should also take the opportunity to communicate regularly with parents/carers on the positive achievements of their children.

recommendation

15. Schools should review the mechanisms and approaches used to communicate with and involve parents/carers in the general life of the school and with their own child's education in particular.

4.11 Parenting is possibly the greatest responsibility which any adult can undertake, and yet most, if not all, people come to the task with little more than their own experiences as a child to help them cope with the many dilemmas which will confront them as parents/carers. Early dysfunction within families can have a considerable negative impact on the development of a child's personal and social development, and consequently on their ability to make a success of school life and beyond. Insufficient attention is attached to the personal suffering and social cost of dysfunctional families. More should be done to identify at the earliest stages, families and children who will need extra support in this respect.

recommendation

16. A national development programme on parenting skills should be developed.

4.12 Establishing a partnership with parents/carers can present both opportunities and challenges. Some parents/carers may feel that they themselves are being blamed for their child's behaviour. They may feel insecure that their child is being criticised, and often the immediate reaction is to jump to their defence. On the other hand, they may feel inadequate if they have struggled over a period of time with the child's behaviour. In either case, parents/carers may feel quite vulnerable in dealing with the school and it is important that this is recognised and steps are taken to deal with it.

4.13 Schools should enter into a joint problem-solving approach with parents/carers and, where appropriate, with young people, at as early a stage as possible – listening to concerns and mutually agreeing strategies for progress.

4.14 There should be an increased emphasis on partnership between schools, families and services providing family support. While the various education, health, social work and community professionals each have a distinctive contribution to make, there is considerable scope for coordinating their work more effectively. Systems of early intervention should be developed to support and sustain the family. The deployment of family support workers by schools would be advantageous.

recommendation

17. The Scottish Executive and local authorities should prioritise funding from within the Excellence Fund to provide for a home-school links worker in secondary schools and primary clusters.

4.15 School Boards and parents' associations have a significant contribution to make towards the development of a positive and inclusive school ethos and in the development of positive behaviour approaches and strategies. They also have a responsibility for involving all parents/carers in the life of the school.

4.16 The DTG believes that there is an increase in parents/carers who may obstruct the school on matters relating to the disciplining of their children. In a small minority of cases, some of these situations can result in verbal and physical attacks on school staff. As a matter of urgency, priority needs to be given to working with all parents/carers in an attempt to establish procedures by which parental concerns may be resolved within a supportive and safe environment.

recommendation

18. A media campaign focusing on parents'/carers' rights and responsibilities in the school system should be established. This should include an information leaflet for parents/carers highlighting these rights and responsibilities, and advising ways to support their child's education

5

supporting pupils in schools

Most children and young people go through school without experiencing any major difficulties. However, some find the experience more challenging than others. It is clear that with appropriate support it is possible to engage all but a tiny minority of pupils in learning and teaching which is appropriate to their needs at that time and also prepares them for later life.

Supporting learning takes many forms. In some cases it will be possible to achieve it by finding alternative ways of working within a mainstream class. From time-to-time, it may be appropriate to establish small group work or one-to-one support. Occasionally it may be necessary to consider alternative provision for children and young people who display particularly challenging behaviour.

Certain groups of children and young people are more vulnerable than others. It is important that schools and education authorities take all steps necessary to ensure that barriers to learning are removed where possible and that social disadvantage is not reinforced by educational disadvantage.

Supporting all children and young people

5.1   Schools may wish to consider how existing in-school services can be integrated to support children and young people's learning and pastoral needs. In primary and secondary schools this may include staff who have been given responsibility for learning support, behaviour support and guidance working much more closely under a collective framework of pupil support.

5.2   In reviewing these services, schools should consider how children and young people are supported to learn effectively and behave appropriately. In offering evidence to the DTG, schools which have already developed an integrated in-school support service considered that they were experiencing significant success with this holistic approach to supporting the needs of pupils.

r e c o m m e n d a t i o n

19.   Schools should give consideration to integrating the work of learning support, behaviour support and guidance into a single overall framework of pupil support in order to achieve a more holistic approach to supporting the needs of all children and young people.

5.3   Learning support teachers play a key role in the development of an effective learning environment for all children and young people. It is clear from the evidence submitted to the DTG that the nature of the work now undertaken routinely by learning support staff, as a matter of course, has mushroomed as a result of schools operating policies of inclusion. Learning support staff are now involved in a much broader spectrum of pupil support rather than the traditionally-held view of learning support in core skills.

5.4   The demands of both the nature and scope of the work undertaken by learning support staff and pressure on their available time is now a matter of serious concern in many schools. Staffing levels for core learning support staff are now considered in some instances to be insufficient to meet the additional demands of the social inclusion agenda. It is the view of the DTG that this matter must be addressed as a matter of urgency. Consideration should be given to increasing the adult/pupil ratio in learning support – both through increasing the levels of teaching staff and special needs auxiliaries.

r e c o m m e n d a t i o n

20.   There should be a review of the criteria and formula for the allocation of learning support staffing to all schools to allow for appropriate levels of support for children and young people with special educational needs, including those with social, emotional and behavioural difficulties.

5.5   Similarly, the demands on the nature of the work of guidance staff in supporting the pastoral needs of a wide range of pupils and families, particularly those with social, emotional and behavioural difficulties, has increased significantly. Guidance staff increasingly carry a much greater caseload of pupils requiring intensive support. This can often have a detrimental effect on their wider responsibilities for curricular and vocational guidance. There must be a review of the role and purpose of guidance in secondary schools. Also, given our findings relating to the importance of early intervention at nursery and primary schools, consideration should be given to a level of guidance provision in primary schools.

r e c o m m e n d a t i o n

21. There should be a comprehensive review of the nature and purpose of guidance, both at primary and secondary school levels, and of the training of guidance staff.

The role of educational psychologists

5.6   The educational psychology service is responsible for providing support to mainstream and specialist educational establishments. In addition, it has statutory responsibilities in relation to referrals from the Reporters' Department and for children who are looked after or accommodated under the terms of the Children (Scotland) Act 1995. Generic work covers children with learning and/or behavioural difficulties from birth to nineteen years of age.

5.7   The key objectives of the educational psychology service include:

- to assess children's needs and plan and evaluate support programmes
- to fulfil statutory duties in relation to recording special educational needs and Children's Hearings
- to provide training courses for teachers and other groups
- to offer a research service and contribute to departmental and school policy.

5.8   The main roles of the educational psychology service involve:

- casework with individual children and their families in conjunction with other agencies
- consultation with staff and parents/carers on general and specific issues relating to both 'referred' and 'non referred' children
- developing and presenting training courses for a range of professionals, including teachers
- involvement in longer-term development work.

5.9   The DTG are of the view that educational psychologists can play a much wider role in promoting positive behaviour in schools. It is important that they look at the environments in which pupils are learning as well as looking at the characteristics of the individual child and his/her personal circumstances outwith the school. This requires close working relationships with schools to develop solution-focused consultancy services and to provide advice on behaviour management. It is important that negotiation of input between the psychological service and schools should achieve a planned and focused involvement which enables joint management of the problem in context. Clear expectations regarding the purpose, nature and outcome of any involvement and respective roles should be agreed.

5.10 Educational psychologists' input is maximised within a structure which encourages professional development and problem solving in the classroom in such a way that it encourages teachers to take into account the whole learning and teaching environment. Such a structure helps determine the roles of support services. It allows a common approach to problems and forms the basis of understanding between the local authority and schools.

5.11 Inclusive schools have been found to involve educational psychologists in joint problem-solving strategies designed at supporting children and young people – which is in contrast to high-excluding schools which often desire external agencies to 'fix' problem-pupils or place them elsewhere.

5.12 Local authority policies and structures are central to determining the nature and role of the educational psychology service. Where the policy is to involve the psychological service in developing the wider authority strategy, this provides a clear rationale for the work of educational psychologists within schools.

5.13 An educational psychologist's time is most effectively used when local authorities have a clearly structured or staged approach to identifying, assessing and responding to young people with difficulties or special needs. A positive feature of such approaches involves seeking advice from educational psychologists at the early stages when a pupil's difficulties are first noticed, through to more direct assessment and intervention at the later stages.

5.14 The DTG is aware of, and concerned about, the apparent national shortage of educational psychologists which is having an adverse impact on the wider and more progressive developments advocated in this report and in the field of education. It welcomes the current review of the educational psychology service in Scotland.

Alternative in-school support

5.15 It is clear that not all pupils can be maintained within a mainstream classroom setting all of the time. There will be occasions for some children and young people where their needs cannot be met in a normal educational setting without affecting the progress and welfare of themselves, other pupils and their teacher(s).

5.16 It is the view of the DTG that children and young people who have social, emotional or behavioural difficulties are pupils with special educational needs. During our visits to schools we were made aware of many excellent examples of mainstream schools managing the balance between progressing the interests of the majority of their pupils, whilst meeting the needs of children and young people who exhibit very challenging behaviour. Primarily through the Government's Alternatives to Exclusion grant scheme, education authorities and schools have developed a range of support systems designed to keep children and young people, who might otherwise have been at risk of exclusion, in school and engaged in purposeful learning and teaching. These strategies include:

- in-class auxiliary support
- the use of behaviour support teachers working with pupils and teachers
- in-school pupil support bases
- involving parents/carers in decision-making.

5.17 Out-of-class facilities should be seen as a short-term strategy to support children and young people during times of difficulty. Their key task should be to plan and implement reintegration strategies to enable the majority of pupils to resume normal class work in as short a time as possible. These facilities may be seen as providing vulnerable children and young people with a relevant education:

- on a short-term, full-time basis as an alternative to exclusion from school
- on a short-term, part-time basis for specific 'hot-spots' during the week
- to support the child to develop skills and attitudes required for appropriate participation in mainstream classes
- as part of a reintegration strategy following an exclusion from school.

5.18 Accordingly, there is a need for schools to be resourced and staff trained to operate in-house, time-out facilities to support children and young people with social, emotional and behavioural difficulties. Such facilities should not become institutionalised and should have as their primary focus the raising of achievement for individual children and confirming or amending the personal curriculum as appropriate. They should also develop approaches which emphasise self-regulation and self-discipline techniques for the child or young person. They should be child-centred in their approach.

5.19 It is important that as part of the preparation for reintegration to mainstream classes, either on a planned part-time or full-time basis, steps are taken to work with the pupil and teacher(s) concerned to ensure that expectations are clearly understood and implemented when the pupil returns. Research and experience shows that where a pupil returns from a pupil support base to a class without sufficient planning and preparation, there is a likelihood that within a very short period of time they may need to return quite quickly to the base. The audit of classroom practice identified under staged intervention in chapter 3 of this report may provide a basis for this planning.

5.20   Well-trained behaviour support teachers with adequate resources, such as on-site places of respite, have clearly made a significant difference to children's behaviour within individual schools. They have also experienced success in providing a consultancy role for class teachers and in developing a model of good practice for working with challenging behaviour.

r e c o m m e n d a t i o n

22. Flexible support provision, including in-class support and facilities to educate children and young people outwith the normal classroom environment, should be established in secondary schools and designated primary schools. Best practice in operating such provision should be further researched and disseminated nationally.

23. In planning for new and refurbished school buildings, local authorities should seek to ensure that suitable and appropriate accommodation is made available for supporting the needs of children and young people who may need to be educated outwith the normal classroom environment. They should also consider how to adapt existing school buildings to allow this to happen.

5.21   Research has shown that time-out facilities can provide a breathing space and coordinated support for individual young people, but that they also have the potential to de-skill classroom teachers and isolate the vulnerable young person. Research is critical of the unclear aims of off-site provision, particularly with its restricted curriculum, the opportunity for poor peer relationships and the subjective and inconsistent way in which children and young people can be selected for them.

5.22   However, a small minority of children and young people may require special educational facilities outwith a mainstream school. Special educational facilities provide an obvious vehicle for effective joint-working and an environment for teachers, social workers, family support workers, psychologists and others to work collaboratively on common programmes for the benefit of individuals and small groups of children. It is essential that all professionals work in a cohesive, holistic and purposeful manner with the aim of restoring the child to mainstream education where this is a realistic target.

5.23   Evidence suggests that the longer a young person spends outside mainstream education, the less likely they will be able to reintegrate into it. The reintegration of children and young people back into mainstream education must be a major priority, and be both properly funded and resourced.

Exclusion from school

5.24 Not only is reintegration an area of concern with children and young people who are moving back to mainstream following some alternative provision, it is also an area of concern in those local authorities where there are permanent exclusions from school. Section 40(3) of the Standards in Scotland's Schools etc. Act 2000 requires that education authorities will provide education for pupils who are withdrawn as a result of being excluded from school. This is better coordinated in some authorities than others – often parents/carers are faced with the daunting task of negotiating directly with schools in an attempt to secure this provision.

5.25 It was also clear to us that some schools appear more willing and open than others to the enrolment of pupils excluded from other schools. This situation is neither desirable nor fair. It is our view that local authorities should not only arrange, but also coordinate all aspects of onward placements in the best interests of the child or young person, and also ensure that there is an equality of commitment from all schools in supporting vulnerable children and young people following permanent exclusions.

5.26 Exclusion from school, either 'temporary exclusion' or 'exclusion/removal from register', should be seen as a last resort and both should be managed within legislative guidelines. These are contained within regulation 4 of the Schools General (Scotland) Regulations 1975, as amended in the Schools General (Scotland) (Amendment) Regulations 1982; section 28H of the Education (Scotland) Act 1980; and sections 40 and 41 of the Standards in Scotland's Schools etc. Act 2000. The publication *Guidance on Issues Concerning Exclusion from School* (Circular 2/98 – Scottish Office, 1998) provides excellent advice for schools and education authorities on the management of exclusions from school. It is clear that not all schools are aware of the requirements of the various pieces of legislation or the procedures contained within Circular 2/98.

r e c o m m e n d a t i o n

24. The guidance contained within Circular 2/98 *Guidance on Issues Concerning Exclusion from School* should be reviewed in the light of the Standards in Scotland's Schools etc. Act 2000. Local authorities should ensure that all schools are aware of relevant guidance and legislation relating to exclusions from school. As part of their inspections of education authorities, HM Inspectorate of Education should review the procedures used to manage the process of exclusions from school.

Looked after children

5.27 Looked after children may live in foster homes, with relatives, friends, in community placements, residential units or schools; most commonly, they live at home under supervision. Under the terms of the Children (Scotland) Act 1995, children are 'looked after' when they are:

- accommodated and/or supervised with the agreement of their parents, and without the involvement of a Children's Hearing
- subject to a supervision requirement made by a Children's Hearing under section 70 of the above Act
- subject to a child protection order, authorisation or warrant
- living in Scotland, but subject to an equivalent order made in England, Wales or Northern Ireland.

5.28 Children can become looked after for a variety of reasons. The majority are likely to come from families who experience stress and hardship because of poverty and other factors related to social exclusion. Some young people become separated from their parents because of such stresses or subsequent family breakdown. Many looked after children will have been affected by distressing and damaging experiences, including abuse or neglect. There is clearly a correlation between such experiences and behavioural difficulties, and this can contribute to a child demonstrating behaviour which is challenging within the classroom. It is worth noting that although only making up just over one per cent of the entire school population, looked after children account for over eight per cent of all school exclusions.

5.29   Significantly, education has the potential to provide all looked after children with an opportunity to improve their life chances and to help them participate fully in society. Schools can provide their only source of continuity and stability in an otherwise turbulent and uncertain world. Schools, individual teachers and support staff can and do make a huge contribution to the stability of the lives of young people in public care. School can provide an environment within which to make friends and learn about relationships, and to receive praise and encouragement. When consulted, children in care repeatedly say that they like school and want to be there – some even describe it as a lifeline.

5.30   Positive educational outcomes can only be achieved through effective joint working involving education and other public agencies. Accordingly, it is a requirement that each local authority has an integrated strategy which brings together education and social work with other appropriate services to ensure positive outcomes for the education of looked after children. This should include how any challenging behaviour might be most effectively managed. This strategy should reflect the local authority's responsibility as a 'corporate parent' for a looked after child. In acting in this capacity, an authority will hold together the many strands in a looked after child's life. The various factors which contribute to a positive experience for looked after children include:

- managing any challenging behaviour within the context of their full life experience
- understanding the importance of education for future life chances
- promoting high expectations
- providing stable and consistent care
- promoting the development of early literacy and numeracy skills
- achieving regular school attendance
- ensuring support from parents and residential/foster carers
- providing ongoing support for further and higher education
- effective joint assessment and planning.

5.31 Having a designated person in each school who maintains an overview of looked after children's progress and takes responsibility for ensuring appropriate measures are in place for supporting their education is critical. It is important that this person plays a key role in developing the school's policy and practice. This designated person should ensure that there is effective communication between the school and carers on matters relating to agreed plans and targets for the child relating to attendance, homework and after-school activities, etc.

recommendation

25. All schools should have a designated member of staff who is responsible for the care, welfare and tracking of progress of looked after children. There is a clear role for this member of staff in supporting colleagues in caring for the interests and welfare of looked after children.

6

multidisciplinary working

It is very rare to find that children or young people who are experiencing problems in school are doing so a result of a single issue. It is usually the case that they are having problems in a number of areas in their lives.

Accordingly, it is important that professionals with a range of different expertise are involved in assessing and supporting the needs of children, young people and their families. It is crucial however, that the approach to multidisciplinary working is well coordinated and managed.

6.1   Children who present challenging behaviour will do so for various reasons, and there is a shared multidisciplinary responsibility to understand such reasons. There will often be a number of contributory factors such as poverty, family stress, abuse, involvement of siblings in similar behaviour patterns or lack of parental control. Schools cannot address these issues alone – they must be addressed through a joint working approach with other agencies.

6.2   Very disruptive pupils are likely to be experiencing difficulty in more than one area of their lives. Any interventions aimed at addressing such behaviours are likely to be just one aspect of the work being undertaken with these children. The false divisions which can exist when concerns are addressed as either a purely social issue or educational issue result both in duplication of effort and lack of coordination.

6.3   Sound partnerships can result in holistic, joined-up approaches to problem-solving. They can have an immediate effect on the quality of life of children and young people, but are more likely to have a cumulative effect, meaning that better outcomes are achieved over a period of time.

6.4   Partnership working with children and young people who present challenging behaviour is just one dimension of effective joint working between agencies. The work of the current Action Team within the Scottish Executive considering better-integrated children's services is due to be published in the autumn of 2001. Its recommendations and the availability of funding through the Changing Children's Services Fund should improve multidisciplinary approaches.

6.5   There is a need for clear roles for the various professionals involved and explicit lines of referral and communication. This can be assisted by the development of a Key Worker system for children at different stages and with different levels of need. This involves an identified professional having lead responsibility, with clear protocols which identify the other professionals who can become involved in the processes of assessment, planning and intervention.

6.6   Inclusive education involves schools working closely with the other agencies involved with children and their families. This is crucial for the promotion of social inclusion for individuals, families and communities. In terms of discipline in schools, the purpose of partnerships is to create a mix of both skills and resources to be directed at positive solutions which:

*   enable the classroom teacher to concentrate on effective learning and teaching

*   enable other pupils to concentrate on learning

*   address the factors which contribute to behavioural difficulties in some young people

*   develop strategies to promote more socially acceptable behaviour.

6.7   The modern children's agenda should seek to avoid the response from social worker or Children's Reporter which dismisses an issue of behaviour in school as being an 'educational' or 'school' problem. Likewise, schools require to develop openness to ideas or solutions which emanate from other professionals. Joyce (2000) suggests five key features of partnership working:

*   creating a partnership agenda

*   selecting an organisational form

*   forming a partnership plan

*   focusing partnerships on achievements

*   developing appropriate skills.

6.8   The management of partnerships requires a range of key factors to be considered and addressed, including leadership – enabling joint decision-making and conflict-management. These are skills which experienced senior managers in schools develop and continuously enhance, and the success of any partnership will require their translation into the arena of multidisciplinary working.

6.9   It is important that partnerships are well planned and founded on clear understandings relating to roles, responsibilities, boundaries, duration and resource issues. Clear mechanisms for dispute resolution are necessary. Partners require to be committed to agreed goals, which must be achievable and regularly reviewed. The organisational commitments must be democratic and avoid hierarchical structures. In developing formal partnerships to address the problems of indiscipline in schools, the issues to be tackled require clear definition and identification. This can be achieved through the shared approach to the assessment of educational needs and multidisciplinary models of service delivery.

6.10   All school staff can make a contribution to developing effective multidisciplinary working. In particular, class and guidance teachers should be encouraged and enabled to participate directly as key members of multidisciplinary teams. They may know the child better than anyone in the school, can pass this understanding on to other professionals and can gain a valuable insight into other parts of the child's life.

School liaison groups/joint assessment teams

6.11   Multidisciplinary working requires a common organisational approach to assessing and supporting needs. The school liaison group (SLG), also known as a joint assessment team (JAT), can provide a coordinating forum for all of the key professionals involved in assessment and planning for individual children. The SLG brings agencies together around the needs of the child or young person. Its make-up will relate to the particular circumstances of the individual or group of schools. It is likely to comprise staff from the school, local social work team, specialist staff such as an educational psychologist and representatives from other organisations such as the police, carers or community education/youth service.

6.12   School liaison groups should meet regularly to consider the needs of identified pupils, including those experiencing behavioural difficulties in school and those at risk of exclusion. They should agree systems and approaches appropriate for assessing the needs of children and young people, and then draw up individual plans and multidisciplinary support packages to address these needs.

recommendation

26.   There should be joint multidisciplinary decision-making relating to the care and welfare of children and young people experiencing social, emotional or behavioural difficulties. Clear mechanisms for ensuring effective multidisciplinary working, adapted to meet local needs and circumstances, should be established for all nursery, primary and secondary school clusters to provide holistic and responsive support for children, young people and their families as required.

Early intervention

6.13 Early, proactive and positive interventions can make very significant differences to the educational, social and personal outcomes for a young person and his/her family. It is our belief that investment in early intervention strategies is more beneficial than later action – either during school years or later in life.

6.14 Effective joint working must take place from the very earliest stage in children's lives, as the earliest interventions are the most likely to be effective. The chances of successful intervention with children and families appear to recede as the child grows older, since behaviours become habitual and expectations of the child lower. Accordingly, there has to be:

* an emphasis on intervention at an early age
* early identification of difficulties at any age, to enable an early and effective intervention.

6.15 The early years are a time of rapid change and development for children. Key transitions, such as going to a care or education setting for the first time, the transition to primary school and from primary to secondary school are all stages when well coordinated support helps children to settle and to succeed in their new environment.

6.16 Child care and early education can provide secure, nurturing, consistent and non-stigmatising environments. Such experiences help prioritise early identification, assessment of needs and active monitoring of young children's attainments. They also provide an opportunity for multidisciplinary preventive support and for raising of the educational achievement of very young children. Accordingly, it is important that services for vulnerable 0 to 3 year-olds are properly coordinated and targeted, and linked with early educational provision.

6.17 Some children enter primary school with established patterns of challenging behaviour. Accordingly, there must be effective joint working within pre-school services across the fields of education, social work and health to ensure that those children who are particularly vulnerable receive coordinated multidisciplinary responses. The Key Worker approach can be particularly helpful in this regard.

6.18 Support to families is particularly important during the early stages in children's lives. The task of bringing up young children is challenging for all parents/carers, but especially so for single parents, those without other family and community supports, families with children with special needs, and those experiencing poverty. Non-stigmatising family support can provide some of the skills, knowledge and additional experiences which assist parents to be empowered to deal with the stress in their lives. Funding has been provided for broad-based support for families with children aged 0 to 3 years through Sure Start Scotland, which seeks to promote a positive start in the lives of very young children to enable them to make the most of later opportunities, such as pre-school education. As at all other times in the life of the child and family, interventions should be designed to help parents and children to devise their own strategies for dealing with their difficulties.

Case Study

Multidisciplinary Working in Gracemount High School

Gracemount High School is a six-year comprehensive secondary school in south-east Edinburgh. It serves a mixed catchment area which includes areas of multiple deprivation as well as owner-occupier housing.

In recent years the school has moved towards a more holistic model of pupil support by integrating much more closely the work of learning support, guidance and behaviour support. The school operates a 'vertical' support structure and house teams consisting of senior management, guidance and learning support staff which meet on a weekly basis to discuss caseloads and strategies. In addition, there is an integrated support team consisting of guidance, learning support and behaviour support staff which meets with the pupil support coordinator on a weekly basis to discuss cross-house issues of pupil support.

There is a pupil support group (PSG) (school liaison group) which consists of house heads, guidance staff, principal teacher of learning support, Gracemount/Liberton Support Team (GLST) Coordinator, school paediatrician, school nurse, educational psychologist, educational welfare officer, social work, City of Edinburgh support unit worker, community education and the community police constable. The PSG meets weekly to discuss planned support and interventions for vulnerable pupils and families. Parents/carers are invited to attend the full PSG, and, where appropriate, smaller sub-groups of the PSG to discuss needs identified and strategies considered appropriate for supporting their children. The educational welfare officer, guidance staff, and in some instances, the GLST staff, will liaise directly with families to provide support in this respect.

The Gracemount/Liberton Support Team (GLST) is a pilot project jointly funded by Education and Social Work working within The City of Edinburgh Council's *Working Together* framework to support vulnerable young people and their families. The aim is to maintain young people in their own homes, schools and communities. It is a multidisciplinary, inter-agency resource with workers from backgrounds in education, social work and community education. It offers a support service to pupils in S1 and S2 from Gracemount and Liberton High Schools and to P7 pupils from the eight feeder primary schools – specifically during their transition into secondary education. A broad range of support is available including:

individual pupil support	family work	group work
in-class support	counselling	transition work
collaborative teaching	consultancy	summer programmes

Access to the service is through school PSGs, the client group being those pupils who are experiencing social, emotional or behavioural difficulties in coping with daily school routine and engaging the curriculum. Commonly these youngsters are at risk of exclusion.

Central to the work of the GLST is partnership with parents/carers in addressing areas of concern and developing appropriate strategies to affect positive change. Equally crucial is ongoing collaboration with school guidance and learning support departments, psychological services, social work and other agencies as appropriate. The level and form of support is determined by individual need and can range from intensive one-to-one contact (as in re-integration of 'school phobic' pupils), through behaviour support group work, to whole-class input (eg., anti-bullying). There is also the facility for joint work with teaching staff and other professionals.

The multidisciplinary approach taken by Gracemount High aims to aid the work of the school in meeting the challenge of inclusion and to support vulnerable families in helping maintain their access to mainstream education.

> **27.** Schools and local authorities should consider how to further enhance their investment in early intervention strategies aimed at pre-school and primary school children and their families. This should include a specific focus on supporting pupils with social, emotional and behavioural difficulties which encompasses local family support strategies.

6.19   Careful attention should always be paid to managing the transition into primary school. Children who have fared well in early education and child care settings may not necessarily adjust easily to school. Children who have had some previous behaviour difficulties may have greater problems in a larger environment which includes a greater range of other children. The primary years offer further opportunities for effective intervention. Many children find primary schools supportive and nurturing environments. Accordingly, primary schools can often manage challenging behaviour which would present greater problems in a secondary setting.

> **28.** Local education authorities and schools should review policies and procedures to ensure all educational transitions, including those between mainstream education and alternative provision, are proactively managed in the best interests of all children, young people and families.

New community schools

6.20 The New Community Schools pilot programme was established in April 1999. The approach now forms an important part of the Scottish Executive's social inclusion and education agendas. The central aim of the initiative is to reduce the barriers to learning faced by many young people in their personal, social and domestic circumstances.

6.21 The rationale and key characteristics of New Community Schools are clearly laid out in the publication *New Community Schools – The Prospectus* (Scottish Office, 1998) which was published prior to the establishment of the pilot programme. New Community Schools must ensure that:

- each child has the fullest opportunity to maximise his or her potential – achievements in all areas must be celebrated, basic skills must be nurtured and developed, self-esteem must be enhanced and high expectations maintained
- full attention is paid to identifying and addressing the child's needs – social, developmental, emotional and health – and their impact on the ability of the child to realise his or her potential
- particular focus is given to the role of the family and parents/carers and the contribution they can make
- teachers, social workers, community education and health professionals operate in an integrated framework to achieve these objectives.

6.22 The New Community School pilot programme has during the past two years seen considerable diversification of models, ranging from some centred on individual schools, to others involving clusters of establishments. The focus varies according to locally determined needs and priorities.

6.23 Effective management of multidisciplinary working in New Community Schools is essential to their success. A model which appears to be developing effectively and has been widely adopted is the appointment of an integration manager who is responsible for coordinating the work of professionals from different agencies within the overall aims of the school.

6.24 The integrated services team and the integration manager need to be viewed clearly as fully recognised members of staff in the school(s) in which they serve. This raises management issues within individual schools and for Directors of Education, Social Work and Health Promotion.

6.25 We consider that the early success of the New Community Schools initiative provides the ideal framework for multidisciplinary working in all schools. We would therefore stress that serious consideration should be given as to how these benefits could be shared further.

r e c o m m e n d a t i o n

29. The success strategies identified in the New Community Schools pilot should be rolled out to secondary schools and primary schools across Scotland.

Advocacy for children and young people in need

6.26 It is recognised that parental involvement in their children's education is a key factor in achieving positive outcomes. The parental role includes having a voice when selecting schools, supporting attendance, making subject choices, homework and work experience. It can include an advocacy role – promoting the child's voice within the school, often when the child's behaviour or the school's responses to it are at issue. One area where advocacy is particularly crucial is where a young person is at risk of exclusion from school or has already been excluded.

6.27 Some children do not have the advantage of such an advocate. They may be looked after, or it may be that their parents do not engage with the school over such matters. Guidance teachers can act as an advocate for all children. Where children are in care, their carers, designated teachers and social workers will have a clear advocacy role, ensuring that they receive the support they need when they need it.

6.28 Children in care, and often those who are not in care, may need an advocate who is not involved in the management of their day-to-day situations. A Children's Rights Officer can perform such a role. This could be an officer employed by the authority, or it may be a service purchased from an independent organisation.

7

working with staff

Staff demonstrate on a daily basis their professionalism and commitment to working with children and young people who display social, emotional or behavioural difficulties. It is important that experienced teachers and new entrants to the profession feel confident, well-prepared and supported in carrying out this challenging work. This is equally important for non-teaching staff.

In order to achieve this staff must be fully involved in making key decisions relating to the formulation and implementation of school policies. They also require access to continuing professional development opportunities which not only enhance their professional competence, but also provide opportunities for accreditation through recognised career development pathways.

Support for Staff

7.1   The negative impact that the problem behaviour of pupils can have on the well-being of adults working with them can itself be serious. A child who has behavioural difficulties can drain the energies and morale of staff and parent/carers. Teachers and school support staff, as well as having responsibilities, have the right to:

- feel fulfilled in the classroom
- be listened to by pupils and colleagues, and taken seriously
- make mistakes and learn from them
- make decisions and use discretion
- have access to relevant information about pupils which may assist with learning and teaching
- expect pupils to engage in learning
- have a quality life outside school
- have their talents and expertise acknowledged
- develop new skills and talents.

7.2   Teachers have an entitlement to support in carrying out their day-to-day tasks. They can be supported through:

- an ethos which incorporates a fair and consistent application of the school's policies on learning and teaching, discipline and pastoral care
- effective middle and senior management
- access to specialist teachers
- access to specialist support staff, including educational psychologists operating in a consultative capacity, trained classroom assistants, trained learning support auxiliaries and other services and agencies
- appropriate developmental opportunities and guidance.

Participation of staff in decision-making

7.3   Teachers and other staff need to develop ownership of the culture, ethos, policies and practices of the school. Teachers should be empowered to make local decisions. There should be an expectation that schools, as learning communities, will be empowered to develop their own local solutions to local difficulties within a framework of local and national accountability.

7.4   Inclusive schools promote trust and responsibility through the sensitive use of relevant pupil information across the professional community involved in the care and welfare of the child – classroom teachers, support staff and related professionals. Whilst the rights of young people to confidentiality must be paramount, school policies should be reviewed to give classroom teachers greater access to information on personal circumstances which may have an impact on a young person's personal and social development, and hence on their learning. Promoted staff in primary schools and guidance staff in secondary schools have a key role to play in supporting teachers and pupils by ensuring that appropriate information on matters relating to the care and welfare of all children is available for class teachers' use.

30. As trusted professionals, all teachers should have access to relevant background information on pupils, including personal and family details, which may affect the learning and teaching process.

7.5   All teaching staff have an entitlement to be part of a wider school community team which supports children and young people experiencing difficulties. This team approach should be part of a support network and will help avoid teachers becoming isolated in dealing with difficult and challenging situations. In some schools first-line guidance is clearly making a difference and could be developed further in all schools.

7.6   Teachers and other staff need opportunities to share their views and feelings with supportive colleagues and managers. In schools where there is peer support for teachers, for example through peer mentoring schemes, professional reflection and self-evaluation is possible, both in a formal and informal capacity. This can support reflective practice at institutional and individual levels.

7.7   There are some schools where Quality Circles, similar to those used in industry, are used by staff to identify good practice, share concerns and solve problems. Effective schools create time for staff to reflect through meetings, during training and in one-to-one exchanges.

7.8   Health at Work schemes, which focus on the well-being of staff, can contribute significantly to raising staff morale, catering for staff welfare and promoting positive lifestyles.

7.9   Staff should have access to professional development opportunities which support participation in the development of self-esteem, trust and relationships. Examples of programmes which have been found useful include assertiveness training, stress management, dealing with difficult people, dealing with conflict situations – all of which are solution-focused rather than reactive.

Initial teacher education (ITE)

7.10 As already indicated in the introduction, the vast majority of young people behave well for most of the time. Thus it is important that students following ITE courses experience programmes of study which reflect this view.

7.11 A wide-ranging review of ITE is currently taking place and it is the view of the DTG that particular attention should be paid to the place of:

- classroom management skills
- promoting positive behaviour
- support for pupils (learning, behavioural and pastoral)
- multidisciplinary working
- promoting pupil participation in decision-making
- working with parents/carers.

r e c o m m e n d a t i o n

31.   The current review of initial teacher education should include the extent to which student teachers are prepared to meet the challenges of supporting social inclusion through effective behaviour management, the promotion of positive discipline and classroom management skills. It should also include the development of opportunities for students following ITE courses to link with professionals in other fields and to develop an awareness of approaches to working with parents and carers.

Continuing professional development (CPD)

7.12 The recommendations relating to CPD within *A Teaching Profession for the 21st Century* (Scottish Executive, 2000) should be fully implemented to ensure an ongoing process of skills development. This will:

- offer educational opportunities to enable people to develop the attitudes and skills necessary for existing/new practices
- maximise opportunities to provide services within schools which integrate support for children and young people and support for learning.

7.13 There should be sensitive, well-publicised systems in place in all authorities to provide practical, non-judgmental support for teachers who experience difficulties with indiscipline. This support must be accessed before difficulties escalate. The nature of this support should be based upon the earliest intervention.

7.14 It is clear from the evidence submitted to the DTG that teachers would welcome the opportunity to have access to quality professional development programmes related to:

- promoting positive behaviour
- behaviour management and support
- improving classroom management skills
- promoting social inclusion at classroom level.

7.15 There should be a national professional development support strategy for teachers which can meet local needs and support managers and staff in whole school approaches to behaviour. The approach should be based on research and staff development materials already in use and linked to the recommended national research strategy in this report.

7.16 There should be a range of accredited professional development programmes from which staff can select to address personal development needs identified through self-evaluation. These programmes should include team working and multidisciplinary training opportunities.

r e c o m m e n d a t i o n

32. In partnership with teacher education institutions and faculties of education, a national continuing professional development programme relating to behaviour management, social inclusion, alternatives to exclusion and effective learning and teaching for probationers, serving teachers and senior managers should be developed.

Multidisciplinary training

7.17 The benefits of multidisciplinary training have long been recognised in specific areas of work with children and young people, such as child protection. The purpose of multidisciplinary training is to achieve shared understanding and to enable more effective joint working. Despite commitment to joint working, existing training and development programmes lend themselves to parallel rather than converging paths.

7.18 Multidisciplinary training should not be seen as one-off, but should be part of a programme of development. Multidisciplinary training should be seen as a critical aspect of:

- initial training
- continuing professional development
- management training.

7.19 At the pre-qualifying stage in the range of multidisciplinary professions, it is important that students are given an opportunity to understand the nature of the responsibilities, professional values and statutory obligations of their colleagues from other agencies. Specific areas of shared knowledge could be usefully presented to health, social work and education students together. Such modules should include child development, learning processes and child behaviour.

7.20 Initial professional training is just that, and there is a need for continuing professional development. CPD programmes should be developed and delivered in a manner which makes them accessible to multidisciplinary training groups in order to build on the approaches to joint working.

7.21 Management development programmes focusing upon multidisciplinary or partnership working should focus on the enhancement gained by strategic thinking across professional boundaries. All multidisciplinary training can be complemented by work shadowing, which helps provide an insight into the values, roles and contribution of other professionals.

recommendation

33. The continuing professional development programme should include opportunities for teaching staff to take part in multidisciplinary training with professionals in other fields and to develop an awareness of approaches to working with parents and carers.

8
conclusion

This report has revealed the nature and extent of the problems of indiscipline in our schools and has highlighted some of the strategies being used successfully in various authorities and individual schools, as well as areas which the DTG feel must be addressed to secure longer-term improvement. It is clear that there is much good work going on in schools across the country and that there are things which can be done at national, authority, school and individual teacher levels to help improve the climate in which teachers teach and children and young people learn.

8.1   There are no easy solutions or quick-fixes available. Improvement requires sustained effort and commitment over a considerable period of time by the wide range of parties who have a direct interest in the education of children and young people, all of which have definite resource implications. It became apparent to us that there were a number of recurring key themes which emerged from all the evidence submitted to us. They were:

- effective vision and leadership
- the importance of high quality learning and teaching
- participation in decision-making by teachers, pupils and parents/carers
- consistency in the implementation and application of agreed policies
- the development of holistic support through multidisciplinary approaches
- the importance of teachers having and sharing high expectations with children and young people
- ensuring that staff who have responsibility for the care and welfare of children and young people are given the time and resources to do this effectively.

8.2   We were aware that schools and individual teachers are concerned about the increasing demands placed upon them as a result of policies linked to social inclusion and alternatives to exclusion. However, it was heartening to know that these concerns were related to the lack of appropriate strategies and resources to embrace social inclusion effectively, rather than a genuine opposition to the principle of giving each and every young person the best possible start in life. We consider it to be inappropriate to set targets for the reduction of exclusions from school by one-third without giving schools the means to achieve this. We would therefore add to our recommendations:

recommendation

34.   The Scottish Executive should develop a set of policy targets linked to the performance measures within the National Priorities, focused on school ethos and discipline. These should support education authorities and schools in maintaining a greater number of children and young people with social, emotional and behavioural difficulties within mainstream schools without adversely affecting the progress or welfare of other pupils or staff. Schools should receive appropriate funding to achieve such targets.

recommendation

35.   The relevant strands of the Excellence Fund should be reviewed and focused on promoting effective learning and teaching, promoting positive discipline and alternatives to exclusion.

8.3   The recommendations laid out in this report provide a range of strategies which we consider will help local authorities and schools support the needs of children and young people and target support and resources more effectively to assist teachers in their work. We hope they provide a framework for improvement. However, the work is just beginning – our task was to highlight the issues and make recommendations – these must now be developed and implemented.

recommendation

36.   There should be a national strategy developed to manage the implementation of the recommendations offered by the Discipline Task Group. Local authorities and schools should also consider how they can best address the recommendations which apply directly to them. HM Inspectorate of Education should review the progress being made by local authorities and schools in this respect through routine inspections.

Appendix 1   Membership of Discipline Task Group

Chairman
Jack McConnell MSP, Minister for Education, Europe and External Affairs.

Members
Bill Alexander, Head of Service (Children, Young People and Families), Highland Council.

Margaret Doran, Head of Schools, Stirling Council.

Joan Fraser, Head of Pupil Support and Inclusion Division, Scottish Executive Education Department.

Evelyn Grant, Reporter Manager, Scottish Children's Reporters Administration, North Region.

Louise Hayward, Assistant Dean Faculty of Education, University of Glasgow.

Ruth Higham, Scottish Parent Teacher Council.

Gordon Mackenzie, Rector, Balwearie High School, Kirkcaldy.

Mukami McCrum, Chief Executive, Central Scotland Racial Equality Council.

Alan McKenzie, Principal Teacher of History, Greenock Academy.

Bill Maxwell, HM Inspectorate of Education, Scottish Executive.

Pamela Munn, Associate Dean Faculty of Education and Professor of Curriculum Research, University of Edinburgh.

Alana Ross, Senior Teacher, Ruchazie Primary School, Glasgow.

Andrew Saunders, Principal, Barnardo's Blackford Brae Project, Edinburgh.

Gordon Stewart, Scottish School Board Association.

Hazel Steele, Head Teacher, Newfields Primary School, Dundee.

Nicol Stephen MSP, Deputy Minister for Education, Europe and External Affairs.

Alastair Struthers, Head Teacher, Lochend Community High School, Glasgow.

Moira Tannock, Head Teacher, Langlaw New Community Primary School, Dalkeith.

David Watt, Acting Assistant Head Teacher, Cleveden Secondary School, Glasgow.

Secretary
Neal McGowan, Head Teacher, Gracemount High School, Edinburgh.

The Discipline Task Group were assisted in their work by Alan Hughes and Helena Wright of the Scottish Executive.

Background

The Scottish Executive is committed to ensuring an education system which enables every child to develop to his or her full potential. Essential to effective learning is that schools that have a positive ethos, classrooms managed by teachers who are properly supported and children who are well-motivated. In the course of the national negotiations on teachers' pay and conditions, a recurrent theme from the teachers' representatives was that teachers are finding it difficult to cope with increasing levels of disruptive behaviour in the classroom. The Scottish Executive therefore decided to establish a Discipline Task Group to examine the issues and to report quickly on ways in which discipline in the classroom can be improved to ensure a quality education for all of our children.

Remit

The remit of the Discipline Task Group was to examine and make recommendations regarding:

- the involvement of teachers in initiatives about discipline
- strategies to deal with instances of indiscipline and bad behaviour
- training for teachers and other staff in the management of bad behaviour in school
- the role of parents in motivating and supporting their children and fostering positive attitudes to education
- the role of other agencies in improving discipline and behaviour.

The Education (National Priorities) (Scotland) Order 2000

The Scottish Ministers, in exercising the powers conferred by section 4(1) of the Standards in Scotland's Schools etc. Act 2000, and after consulting education authorities and giving such persons as appear to them to have an interest in the matter an opportunity to make their views known, hereby make the following Order a draft of which has, in accordance with section 4(2) of that Act, been laid before, and approved by resolution of the Scottish Parliament.

Interpretation

In this order –

"literacy" means competence in reading and writing (including word-processing) and understanding and appreciating different types of texts including literary texts and an ability to precise material in a logical order; and

"numeracy" means competence with numbers and using graphical skills to interpret and communicate quantifiable information (including facility with graphs, symbols, diagrams and calculators), and in applying numerical and other mathematical and statistical skills in everyday and more abstract concepts.

National Priorities (2000)

The National Priorities in Education for the purposes of section 4(1) of the Standards in Scotland's Schools etc. Act 2000 are –

(1)   to raise standards of educational attainment for all in schools, especially in the core skills of literacy and numeracy, and to achieve better levels in national measures of achievement including examination results

(2)   to support and develop the skills of teachers, the self-discipline of pupils and to enhance school environments so that they are conducive to teaching and learning

(3)   to promote equality and help every pupil benefit from education, with particular regard paid to pupils with disabilities and special educational needs, and to Gaelic and other lesser used languages

(4)   to work with parents/carers to teach pupils respect for self and one another and their interdependence with other members of their neighbourhood and society and to teach them the duties and responsibilities of citizenship in a democratic society

(5)   to equip pupils with the foundation skills, attitudes and expectations necessary to prosper in a changing society and to encourage creativity and ambition.

Children (Scotland) Act (1995), Edinburgh: The Stationery Office.

The Disabled Persons Act (1986), London: HMSO.

HM Inspectorate of Education (2001) *Alternatives to Exclusion from School,* Edinburgh: The Stationery Office.

Joyce, P. (2000) *Strategy in the Public Sector,* Chichester: Wiley.

Ofsted (1996) *Exclusions from Secondary Schools 1995/6,* London: The Stationery Office.

Scottish Executive (2000) A *Teaching Profession for the 21st Century* – The report of the Committee of Inquiry into professional conditions of service for teachers, Edinburgh: The Stationery Office.

Scottish Office (1996) *How good is our school?,* Audit Unit, HM Inspectors of Schools.

Scottish Office (1998) *New Community Schools – The Prospectus,* Edinburgh: The Stationery Office.

Standards in Scotland's Schools etc. Act (2000), Edinburgh: The Stationery Office.

Tinklin, T., Croxford, L., Ducklin, A. and Frame, B. (2001) *Gender and Pupil Performance in Scottish Schools,* University of Edinburgh.

Warnock, M (1978) *Special Educational Needs: Report of the Committee of Enquiry into the Education of Handicapped Children and Young People,* London: HMSO.